George Perkins

The tariff

Speech of George C. Perkins of California in the Senate of the United

States

George Perkins

The tariff

Speech of George C. Perkins of California in the Senate of the United States

ISBN/EAN: 9783337154585

Printed in Europe, USA, Canada, Australia, Japan

Cover: Foto ©Suzi / pixelio.de

More available books at **www.hansebooks.com**

AN AMERICAN POLICY, AN AMERICAN MARKET, AND AMERICAN WAGES FOR THE FARMER AND WORKMAN.

The American protectionist does not seek to evade the legitimate results of his theory. He starts with the proposition that whatever is manufactured at home gives work and wages to our own people, and that if the duty is even put so high as to prohibit the import of the foreign article, the competition of home producers will rapidly reduce the price to the consumer.—*James G. Blaine.*

THE TARIFF.

SPEECH

OF

HON. GEORGE C. PERKINS,

OF CALIFORNIA,

IN THE

SENATE OF THE UNITED STATES,

Thursday, April 19, 1894.

WASHINGTON.
1894.

SPEECH

OF

HON. GEORGE C. PERKINS,

OF CALIFORNIA,

IN THE SENATE OF THE UNITED STATES,

Thursday, April 19, 1894.

The Senate, as in Committee of the Whole, having under consideration the
bill (H. R. 4864) to reduce taxation, to provide revenue for the Government,
and for other purposes—

Mr. PERKINS said:

Mr. PRESIDENT: One of the most difficult problems of national
legislation is to enact laws that shall be in harmony with the intelligent thought of the people from all portions of this vast
Republic; from the northern line to the Gulf of Mexico; from
the extreme west to the eastern boundary. A diversity of interests must ever characterize a country so vast in extent as ours,
and this fact should imbue us with charity for the opinions of
those who differ with us. We are each of us, to a greater or
less extent, influenced by our environments and local interests.
But aside from all these differences growing out of divergent
localities, there is one point upon which all intelligent and patriotic Americans at least should be able to agree, and that is
upon the necessity for an American policy upon all questions of
citizenship, of taxation, and, as far as possible, of finance.

Love for our Country and her Institutions.

We should have no other political creed but love for our common country and her institutions. The stability of nations, of
empires, of dynasties, is grounded in the selfishness of their ad-
herents and supporters. So true is this, and so generally ac-
knowledged, that it has become almost axiomatic that nations
are strong in proportion as they are selfish. Under the present
order of things the question that conserves the highest degree
of welfare for us should be paramount in our affections, even
though other nations would gladly have it otherwise. Protection of our homes, of our industries, and the elevation and dignity of labor should be the principal cardinal doctrine of every
patriotic American citizen. The question of expense and revenue is a very simple one that comes home to each member of
every community, and the same rule that applies to us as individuals must govern us collectively, whether organized into a
municipality, a State, or a nation.

A Business Proposition to be Considered.

Is it not then a plain business proposition, divested of all specious pleading, that we have before us for consideration? It requires in round numbers say $500,000,000 per annum to properly carry on this Government. That is, we must provide that much money for the expenses of the legislative, judicial, and executive departments of the Government. The support of the Army and Navy, diplomatic service. coast fortifications, river and harbor improvements, public buildings, light-house and life-saving service, pensions and hospitals, interest on public debt, scientific research, and other purposes, all intended for the benefit, advancement, and honor of this great Republic. This large sum of money must be obtained either by direct or indirect taxation. It must all come from our own people, and from those that do business with us from other countries, selling us the products that come from their soil, or that which is manufactured by the skill or labor of foreign workmen.

Our people pay their taxes for the support of municipal, county, State, and National Government; and, in addition thereto, they must pay a special license for conducting the business in which they are engaged. Why then should we permit foreign nations to bring here, without paying for the privilege, their products and wares to compete with our industries. giving them equal if not better advantages than our own people. We have a land extending through many degress of latitude and longitude that is capable of producing everything known to the vegetable kingdom, while our mines of mineral wealth are diversified and practically inexhaustible. We honor labor as the source of all wealth, and it is the labor of American manhood that has developed the resources of the country and is to-day its power and safety.

How to Raise the Revenues.

It has been the policy and plan, for the past thirty years, of wise American statesmanship to raise about one-half of the expense of the Government by placing an import duty upon the products of other lands that come into this country for consumption or use of our people, and to so adjust these duties that they will best protect and foster American industries, and thereby dignify and protect American labor against the cheap, servile, and contract labor of foreign lands. That this is the correct principle is evidenced from the fact that during this time our industrial interests have been stimulated and our people prosperous, contented, and happy.

The Wilson Tariff Bill.

The bill before us for consideration, designated a tariff for revenue, proposes to take from the import duties $75,000,000, which is simply a license the producer pays for the privilege of entering into our home market with his merchandise on equal terms with one to the manor born, and impose this additional burden upon our own people in the form of increased excise duty and an income tax upon the gain or profit made by their diligence, industry, and enterprise. When we consider this contemplated change and remember the deep interest taken by England and other European powers in our late Presidential election, with what force does the prophetic words of Thomas Jefferson come home to us when he said:

The election of a President of America some years hence will be much more interesting to certain nations of Europe than ever the election of a King of Poland was.

When in periods of great financial crisis, due to or affected by the action of government, it becomes the duty of all officers of the government to inquire into any and all causes for the disturbance of the business affairs, to promote the prosperity of our people, to add to their comfort and strengthen their power, and to do all these things unbiased by personal or local interests and untrammeled by party affiliations.

The Trouble and the Remedy.

After these investigations it becomes our duty to set forth the causes leading to our conclusions and state the remedies, if found. Actuated by an earnest desire for the general welfare of our entire country, and regarding the question of national finance as a purely business question, I hope to discuss it as a business man from a broad business basis.

The fact is conceded that a general depression in business prevails over our entire country, enterprise stagnant, labor unemployed, the revenues of Government lagging behind the expenditures, the debt increasing and national bankruptcy impending. This in a time of peace with the world, in a time of general health and a period of unusual agricultural and mineral productiveness, presents a condition that may well be denominated a crisis. This condition in the United States is attributed to changes and threatened changes of our revenue laws and the violent partisan agitation thereof.

How to Support the Government.

There are many theories of methods for the acquisition of means for the support of government: as a single tax upon land; the issuing of mortgage bonds on land; a direct tax, consequent upon free foreign trade; internal revenue, or tax upon home products, manufactures, business transactions, inheritances, incomes, and prosperity; governmental ownership of railroads, canals, and inland water ways; in the transmission of telegraphic and telephonic messages; in the business of banking and exchanges connected with its postal system; and by levying a uniform duty on imports without any variation or discrimination whatever; our plan, the Republican plan, of levying duties with discriminations designed to protect American industries and products, to foster American manufacture, to develop American resources, to lighten the burdens of taxation of the busy and industrious classes; to exact as far as possible a toll from the foreign producer or manufacturer upon the goods and wares imported in competition with like goods and wares of home production or manufacture.

A System of Schedules of Disputes.

Such are some of the different methods proposed by theorists and parties in our country. Other countries have other methods of land rentals, mining royalties, business monopolies, and many devices for the acquisition of revenue. As business men we should discuss and enlighten ourselves on all the methods devised by theorists or statesmen. and, after thorough and impartial examination, adopt that which is most equitable and practicable, accomplishing the purpose in view of giving revenue and fostering our general welfare. While the many theories have their advocates, with books written, conventions held, and

1257

parties formed in their interests, there has but one been presented for our discussion at the present time, and this presents but a system of schedules for dispute.

The Various Kinds of Tariffs.

We have been accustomed to hear much about a tariff for revenue without discrimination as the only constitutional tariff, and a tariff for revenue with discrimination, and upon these distinctions the American people divided into parties in the early part of this century. These were the tariffs for revenue and the tariff for protection. The first was the theories upon which was based the Democratic party and the latter the basis of the Whig party, and maintained by the Republican party. Upon these many battles of the hustings and the forum have been fought, and over the failure of one and the triumph of the other has the country been agitated, its business depressed or promoted. These propositions were well defined in the platform of the two, yes, three or four, political parties in the last general campaign, and these were expected to be discussed in this Congress. But we have wandered far away from our course.

The Democratic party has fallen from its high estate, abandoned its principles utterly, and instead of making open and bold war upon its ancient doctrines and adopted platform, enters beneath the Republican platform, attacks the Republican tariff measure which it declared unconstitutional and a robbery, and tearing it down attempts to build on the same principles a weaker structure from the same materials. We are thus brought to this strange contest, with no great fundamental principle to investigate, but to contrast as a measure of polity the legitimate with the illegitimate, the complete with the incomplete, the strong and carefully completed structure with that made of the madly gathered and weakened fragments.

The Difference Between Them.

The questions we have before us are denominated the Wilson bill and the McKinley bill, or rather the amendments to and reconstruction of the latter. The McKinley tariff was a growth of thirty years' experience, modified after many years of careful study, and with some amendments. would be perfected in its general scope so that it would provide sufficient revenue with the least possible burdens, thereby giving the best encouragement to commerce and the greatest possible protection to home people and to home industries. With this evolution by years of the protection tariff system under the guidance of men of great business discernment. pure patriotism, extending its beneficence over every section, State, country, hamlet, and farm of the Union, holding firm that which is our own, by ourselves, and for ourselves, enhancing our prosperity and strengthening our strength, we ask that it be maintained as a whole and that which is experimental, protective in principle, yet confessedly ineffective in its protection, claiming to seek revenue. yet admitted to fall far short of obtaining requisite revenue be quickly and utterly rejected.

The Interest of California in the Bill.

In discussing the question of tariff or protection, of mutual assistance, national development, and national revenue, it may appear selfish to advocate the special interest or interests of a single State, but of California interests I will speak, as they affect the whole. One knowing California can not speak of her without enthusiasm; vast in area, grand in scenery, genial in climate; almost every mineral known to man, often beneath a soil of great fertility or in mountain rocks or desert plains; a State of such varied and unlimited natural resources that she could be inclosed in a Chinese wall of impenetrability and possess within herself all the necessities and luxuries of life, all the raw materials used in manufactures, the facilities of manufacture, the means of defense, the money of commerce, and all that goes to make a rich and powerful people. But California is an integral part of this fraternal Union, the western buttress of this mighty Government, sharing in all the hopes, glories, burdens, and responsibilities of her sister States. So illimitable are her resources that she can claim preëminence in agriculture, horticulture, viticulture, and minerals. Of the latter, only the most experienced of scientists can rehearse the catalogue.

The Resources of California.

California is vast in area and illimitable in resources, and over all is the most genial and salubrious climate known in civilized lands. With an area of 158,360 square miles, equal to 101,350,400 acres, she has but 1,208,130 inhabitants, as shown by the last census. Excluding deserts and lofty mountain ridges, there is remaining an area larger than all Great Britain and Ireland, which, acre for acre, possesses resources equal if not superior, and can maintain as dense a population in much greater comfort and attain a greater wealth. This vast area we want developed. You want it developed. You want its products and we want your products. We want many millions of people where we now have so few. We want, however, American citizens in the true and patriotic interpretation of the name!

Besides the minerals, California in 1892 produced 39,157,000 bushels of wheat, 13,000,000 bushels of barley, 6,000,000 bushels of corn, 33,000,000 pounds of wool, 2,000,000 gallons of brandy, 20,000,000 gallons of wine, 22,000,000 pounds of beet sugar, and 35,142,969 pounds in 1893, the entire beet-sugar product of the United States being 44,953,264 pounds.

The Fruit Industries of the State.

California exported, chiefly to the East, in 1892, 112,749,200 pounds of fresh deciduous fruit, 69,715,000 pounds of citrus fruit, 59,432,661 pounds of dried fruit, 53,336,960 pounds of raisins, 110,-574,420 pounds of canned fruit, and 4,126,605 pounds of almonds and walnuts. The development of these industries which have afforded these exports has been aided by protection, which should be enlarged rather than diminished. As the production of the semitropic fruits in our country has increased the price has declined and the consumption kept pace with the production. The fact is also established that our oranges, lemons, figs, raisins, currants, olives and olive oil, almonds, and walnuts are equal in quality to the best and superior in general to the like products imported.

But California contends at a disadvantage with the old and populous country of the Mediterranean, of cheap labor, low rates of interest, and cheap transportation. Over mountains and deserts the California products must be carried, but notwithstanding these hardships the East is supplied with fruit of better quality and lower rates than formerly, when the foreign market had the monopoly. Yet with this great product not one-fifth of the people of the United States enjoy the luxury of semitropic fruits and nuts. We ask that the prevailing duties on these be not disturbed, and that the bill under consideration be so amended that these industries may continue to develop and increase.

The home production of semitropic fruits appears to have largely increased their consumption. Formerly rare and costly luxuries, they are coming into more common use, and we may look forward to the time when they will become common but cheap luxuries to all classes of people. That this is a desideratum devoutly to be wished no one will deny, and it may be accomplished under just protection. The value of olive oil imported in 1881 was $480,683 for 384,412 gallons, and in 1891, under an increased duty, was $876,613 for 733,489 gallons.

The Semitropical Fruits.

In the meantime the production in California has largely increased, and is now marching on to a business of great magnitude, olive orchards being planted in every section of the State. Pickled olives were imported in 1891 to the value of $320,163. This commodity is proposed to be placed on the free list. California given protection will supply the demand with a better article, and in time at less rates. The importation of dried prunes has averaged 60,000,000 pounds annually during the past seven years. California produced in 1886, 2,000,000 pounds, and in 1892, 25,000,000 pounds, the consumption steadily increasing as the good quality of the California product becomes known, at the same time lessening the price of the consumer.

Why the Encouragement Should Continue.

There was imported into the United States in 1892, 23,250,809 pounds of raisins, and California in the same year sent to the Eastern markets 53,336,960 pounds. This fruit is still classed among the luxuries, used only by the more wealthy, but under the stimulus of home production is advancing to common use and becoming a necessity in the household. But not one-tenth of the amount is consumed that will be under the full development of American production. Let the encouragement of American production continue, and all the various sections of our country, the Atlantic coast, the great Valley of the Mississippi, the mining region of the Rocky Mountains, and the high plateaus will all be supplied abundantly with a better article and at cheaper rates than have ever before been known. American production of raisins, as of other delicate fruits, means prosperity to large American communities and adding an increased ratio to the aggregate American wealth, in this, that it saves to the people for circulation and mutual assistance what would otherwise go abroad not to return in any form, and that it gives to capital investments for its money, to bankers activity in their exchanges, employment to labor, freight for transportation, markets for manufactures and farm products, building up cities, communities, and States.

Bold and enterprising men have engaged in these productions, investing large sums of money and the toil of years until now tens of thousands of people and millions of dollars are represented. A vast amount of wealth has been added to the country, and comfort and luxuries given the people. To establish this and to advance it protection was necessary, and no free trader nor pessimist can show that it has worked any hardship in America. In fact, in this case, protection has proven an unexceptional blessing. The duty upon the importation of raisins and other semitropical fruits should be retained as established in the tariff of 1890. This also affords the opportunity to increase the revenue where the foreigner will pay for the privilege of competing in the market. The high prices we have paid for these delicacies have enriched the landowners of the Mediterranean countries at the cost of ours stores of the precious metals.

The Specialties of California.

These may be called some of the specialties of California and the list be greatly enlarged. Of these specialties, citrus fruits, figs, raisins, and nuts, we imported in 1891 to the value of $15,062,208, and in 1892 to the value of $11,237,285. This was so much money sent abroad that could have aided in passing over the period of hard times if it had been retained at home in exchange for home products of the same class. The encouragement of the cultivation of these fruits opens another source of business for our people. This is in the preservation of fruits for exportation. This also implies the encouragement of sugar production.

Statistics show that Great Britain consumes annually per capita 70½ pounds of sugar, while but 55 pounds are used in the United States. It is also known that the table consumption in the United States greatly exceeds per capita that in Great Britain. The excess in the latter country is used in the preservation of fruit and the making of the various commodities, as jams, jellies, and other articles of which fruit is the basis.

This indicates the enormous business now existing in England in this line, and what a great industry may be developed in our own country by the encouragement of the culture of fruit and sugar.

What California has Produced.

Of gold California has given $1,300,000,000 to the world, revolutionizing commerce and constituting the chief factor in creating the golden era in which we live. California now produces $12,250,000 of the precious metals annually, of which over $11,000,000 is gold, the entire gold product of the Union being $33,000,000. But large as is California's output of gold there are many other minerals of great importance to the country that are affected by the tariff. I will name a few of the industries affected.

The Borax Industry.

Of these one is borax. The history of this mineral, its ancient rarity and value, the discovery of it in California and Nevada in peculiar forms, the heroic development of its production, the cheapening of its price, and the beneficence it has proven to the world constitute one of the most interesting chapters in mineralogy. The mineralogists of California, incited by the discoveries of gold in great abundance, turned their attention to other useful minerals, the search for borax being one, and from traces observed in the analysis of water followed the clue until the object sought was found.

At the date of this discovery the common price of borax was 50 cents a pound, and its uses were limited. Tuscany, in Italy, was then the chief source of supply. Following this discovery borax was found in different forms in the deserts of Nevada and Eastern California. Following these, borax, in similar formations, was found in Asiatic Turkey and in other countries. But the Americans had led the way. In the search and exploitation of the borax fields our miners of the West have penetrated the most inhospitable deserts of the world, and through years of toil, hardships, and danger have shown an enterprise and courage worthy of the highest reward.

Paid the Government for the Land.

They have not made the desert to blossom as the rose, but they have redeemed its character to such an extent that they have paid the Government many thousands of dollars for the land, extracted from it many millions of dollars of value, cheapened a product to domestic, artisan, and scientific uses, made possible and developed new and important industries. In this they have made the barren deserts great and valuable factors in the progress, comfort, and commercial affairs of the world. Of these desert fields where borax is found the most famous is the historic Death Valley in Eastern California, a valley deep below the level of the sea although surrounded by the high plateau of the Great Basin and within view of the highest land in the United States.

The region belongs to and is characteristic of the eastern base of the Sierra Nevada mountains, a region of unique formation, abounding in useful minerals usually denominated salts, as well as silver, lead, and other metals. It is a region of excessive heat in summer, and in winter is reached only through the deep snows of surrounding mountains. Of the horrors of this inhospitable region it is unnecessary to tell, but brave men have penetrated it hundreds of miles from railroads, have developed stores of wealth, have established outposts of civilization, opening markets for agricultural and manufactured products, and, if these mining industries are not destroyed by un-American and hostile legislation there will be opened lines of railroad through the country, and another desert region will be eliminated from the map.

The Bill Destroys the Industry.

Destroy this industry, as the Wilson bill proposes, and these bright hopes of the future are obliterated, the business of invested capital bankrupted, thousands of men deprived of labor, country revenues cut off, and the people of the United States made to pay the foreign manufacturer and importer an exorbitant increase over the present price for an article now in common use. That this prediction of increased price has a basis we have but to look to the past. The English obtained control of the Turkish borax mines. While England never rejects ripened fruit ready to fall into her lap, she does not always wait for it to fall, but shakes the tree, and then if it will not fall reaches for it and pulls it down. So England got the concession of the Turkish and other borax mines, and having free entrance to the American market, proceeded to undersell and close out the American borax miner. When this was so nearly accomplished that English manufacturers had control of the market the price was put up to 15 cents per pound. Then came the tariff of 1882, and the year following the price fell to 10 cents per pound, the fall in price being the full amount of the duty, and the American business revived. This is an example of the benefit of a protective tariff to our people and the producer.

Gen. Rosecrans, a distinguished and learned gentleman and a Democrat, in presenting this question to Congress in 1883, recommended duties on pure boracic acid, 10 cents per pound; on commercial boracic acid, 8 cents per pound, and on other forms of borax, 5 cents per pound. The bill now under consideration places borax on the free list, and to this treatment of a great industry I earnestly and decidedly object and protest. The world's production of borax is about 24,000 tons annually, the United States producing 7,000 tons; Italy, 3,000 tons; Turkey, 9,000 tons; Thibet, 2,000 tons; Chile, Bolivia, and Peru, 3,000 tons.

This product has increased from a few thousand tons since the discovery in California and Nevada until the present time, when about 9,000 tons of borax is used annually in the United States. The uses to which it is put are various. One of the oldest was by the blacksmith in welding iron, and as a medicine and emollient sold by the druggists, but since it is so largely produced its uses have multiplied a hundredfold.

We Should Protect American Borax.

Now it is important in calico printing and dyeing, in painting, blacking, washing, enameling of porcelain, glazing in potteries, flux in smelting. an antiseptic and preserver of flesh, a substitute for soap, a disinfectant, and many other purposes, entering the ordinary household as a necessity. The working of the desert borax fields involves the labor of several hundred hardy men, with great teams of twelve to twenty animals each, maintaining stations, supplying refining works, giving transportation to railroads and consuming a large amount of the products of the farm, manufactories, and mechanical shops of the country. The enemies of protected industries lay much stress upon opening markets in foreign countries for American products. I would ask if by purchasing the Turkish, Thibetan, and Bolivian borax the miners of those countries would consume as much of American products, patronize American blacksmiths, American wagonmakers, or American railroads as do the American borax miners.

The other Minerals of the State.

Among other minerals found abundant in California are chromium, antimony, quicksilver, manganese, sulphur, salt, niter, soda, potash, gypsum, onyx, alabaster, lime, marble, and others, and all varieties of these which enter largely in the arts, manufactures and domestic uses, and are commodities of great commercial importance. All these are proper subjects for tariff for revenue, and such tariff would afford incidental protection and therefore assist in the development of American resources and American industries. Chromium, chromic iron, or, as commonly called, chrome, is used in making coloring matter for silks, cotton, woolens, wall paper, carpets tanning leather, and other purposes, and its uses are increasing. This mineral exists in all the mountain ranges of the Pacific coast from Puget Sound to the Mexican line, and was formerly mined with fair profit, some 4,000 or 5,000 tons being shipped annually to the Atlantic coast, but since the removal of import duties the business has nearly ceased. A duty of 25 per cent would both aid the revenue and revive the industry on the Pacific coast. Now chrome is imported from Australia, Scotland, and Turkey in exchange for gold. Develop this resource and stop another leak for our gold.

Antimony is used largely in a great variety of manufactures, and of this mineral we have sufficient for all our needs. All that can be said regarding chromium is applicable to antimony. With a duty upon its importation, attention would be given to the abundant stores of it in our own country, and soon the metal would be cheapened.

Quicksilver.

Of quicksilver California has already produced $60,000,000, and large capital is invested in its mining and reduction. While there is still an abundance in the many mines of California the exceedingly rich deposits have been exhausted, and the industry may be entirely destroyed if the product of the foreign mines is permitted to enter into competition free of duty. All the foreign mines of quicksilver are or have been owned or controlled by the Rothschilds, and it would not be wise American policy to transfer so important a mining industry to that wealthy and monopolizing house. The foreign producers will sell their quicksilver for gold or for bonds, payable, principal and interest, in gold, and for nothing else.

Of the extent of the quicksilver deposits in California, or of the capital invested in mines and reduction works, there is no question nor speculation; nevertheless all this property and this vast resource and plant for home labor, home production, and home consumption of farm products and domestic manufactures may be destroyed by the unfettered competition of foreign capital based on foreign low rates of interest and cheap labor. Heretofore quicksilver has had a protection of 10 cents per pound duty, but now it is proposed to admit it free. Such a policy can not be defended. No one can show a manufacture hampered or an industry of any class burdened by the high price of quicksilver under the present conditions, nor can any one promise that quicksilver will be cheaper when the American mines are closed by foreign competition. There would be no industries or manufactures retarded were the price of this mineral double what it now is. The gold and silver mines of the West have been the chief consumers of this valuable useful liquid metal, but an unfortunate policy has so borne upon these that quicksilver mining has received an almost fatal blow.

Congress Should not Finish it.

I hope that Congress will not give it the finishing stroke. This is an industry of but a single and distant State, for quicksilver is found in no other part of our country, excepting California, in sufficient quantities to pay for working. The Senators from New York or Alabama may not now realize that its life or death affects them. A manufacturer of New York may, temporarily, obtain quicksilver at a slightly reduced rate, but no consumer will ever see the reduction. The gain to the importer is infinitesimal at best, but the loss to California is serious. California is but a unit of the Republic, but of units the whole is made. The prosperity of the whole is in consequence of the prosperity of singles, and the infliction of injury upon one has a widespread and baleful influence upon all. Quicksilver is peculiar in many things, and particularly for the fact that it is produced in only four parts of the world. Its sources of production are Spain, Austria, Italy, and California.

The History of the Metal.

The Almedan mine in Spain was discovered over two thousand years ago; the Idria in Austria, four hundred years ago, while the mines in Italy were discovered over a hundred years ago. The latter, however, play no very important part in the industry, as they produce but a small quantity comparatively. The cinnabar or sulphide of mercury, from which quicksilver is produced, was discovered in California in 1850. The discovery of gold there only a short time previous hastened the development of the industry. The price of quicksilver then was $1.50 per pound. To-day it is less than one-third of that amount. Had it not been for the quicksilver industry in California there would have been no competition in prices and hardly any conjecture can be made as to what the ruling price would be, for, as I have stated, the quicksilver of the world outside of that of California is controlled by one corporation or firm. In 1878 there were thirty quicksilver mines in the State of California, while to-day there are not ten—prices have steadily declined; the mines could not be worked to any degree of profit. The United States is one of the largest consumers of the metal.

The production of quicksilver is already hampered with many difficulties, but this proposed action to place it on the free list consummates them all. The cost of production is nearly three times as large as that of the mines of Spain and Austria, for the reason that there is a better grade and a higher paid class of labor necessary. The price obtained to-day is barely sufficient to keep the mines running, and striking off the protection of 10 cents per pound simply gives the foreign producer the absolute market and the control of the price. It benefits the great financial house of the Rothschilds, but it throws out of employment and leaves idle our American workmen. It is a strange policy for us to adopt, to close down our own mines to oblige those who control the only other three sources of production, and they in Europe. It seems to me that it can not be defended and that it is as uncalled for as it is unjust.

Duty Does Not Injure the Consumer.

The American consumer of quicksilver has not been injured and will not be by the existing law. The protective tariff has helped to keep the quicksilver mines of California running, and they, and they alone, have reduced and kept down the price to the consumer. A gentleman who is connected with the quicksilver production in California says of the case as follows:

The amount produced in this country is equal to its need at present. But little has been imported for a long series of years since the imposition of the duty, and during this past year none at all.

I beg to call your attention to the fact that were the mines of California to be closed down, as they must inevitably be unless some protection is afforded, that the whole power of making the price would lie with the Spanish and Austrian Governments, as represented by their agents, the Rothschilds, and we should be at their mercy. When this duty has been so slow as to cause a shut-down of the American mines, this has been the case heretofore. We are now protected by a duty of 10 cents per pound. This is little enough, and we ask in consideration of the capital involved, and the labor of 5,000 men employed at good wages, that it be kept at the present rate.

The Sugar Industry.

Let us for a moment consider the question of sugar; its importation: costs to our people; as a means of revenue, and the effects of its production at home. Let us look upon it from the Democratic standpoint of free trade and from the Republican standpoint of an assisted industry either by protection or bounty. The McKinley bill removed the tariff duty from raw sugar, but to foster its production as a domestic industry enacted that a bounty equivalent to the former protection be paid for a limited period to the home manufacturer. The bill as it came to the Senate takes no notice of sugar as a means of revenue, nor offered protection or assistance. Originally it proposed a sliding scale of bounty, but that was stricken out. Common justice demands that a contract made by the Government with her citizens should be observed in perfect good faith, therefore the policy of the bounty should prevail until such time as that named in the act or the American sugar industry fully commands the market.

The American people now pay annually to foreign countries an excess of $100,000,000 for sugar produced by servile and coolie labor or in countries where the production is assisted by government. The consumption in the United States is about 2,000,000 tons per annum, nearly all imported, on which was formerly paid between $50,000,000 and $80,000,000 revenue to the Government in addition to the amount paid the foreign producer, the shipper, the importer, and the trusts, who held the consumer at their mercy, a total cost of unrefined sugar to the people of over $230,000,000, taking the average rate of sales at commercial centers.

For the product of sugar in the last year in this country there was paid on the bounty fund over $9,000,000, the exact figures being $9,375,130.88. The Senator from Indiana [Mr. TURPIE] yesterday in discussing this question stated that $15,000,000 had been paid. I find, however, that his figures are not in accord with those of the Secretary of the Treasury, as he reports but $9,000,000. The question before us is, which is of more benefit to the people, the fostering of this industry or its destruction?

A Simple and Feasible Way of Raising Revenue.

There can be no question that sugar by importation affords a most simple and feasible means of raising a large revenue. So do tea and coffee. So a great revenue could have been obtained from the sale of the public lands, the ownership of the salt and other mines, as do some countries, and as was formerly advocated in this. But with the progress of enlightenment, better democracy and greater liberality has obtained. Our mines are owned and worked by the people and their prosperity has resulted; our public lands have become the homes of independent farmers and populous and prosperous States have grown up. The tax upon tea and coffee was removed to lighten the burdens of the poor classes, and all rejoiced in the beneficent act.

Then came another step forward in the same direction and the tax was taken from sugar and all those classes of people who feel the burdens of the purchases of the comforts and necessaries of life felt the relief and were made glad. In all these times and with all the apparent sacrifices of the Government, all wrung from it with terrible opposition, the revenues were maintained, the country prospered in accelerated ratio, and the people were benefited. Here we might contrast the simple or barbarous methods of levying duties with the discriminating or enlightened. Tea and coffee, the luxuries of the industrial classes, competed with nothing produced at home and were beneficently exempted from taxation.

Why the Bounty is Imposed.

Sugar, entering into a vast number of comestibles and commodities, and as much of a necessity to the poorer classes as tea and coffee, is an importation in competition with a domestic product in a small way, but may be entirely produced at home. To cheapen it to all classes, to aid in the preservation of our fruits, and to assist manufactures, the tax was removed. But one of our great States was largely devoted to its production and to leave it to the unbridled competition of the foreign product of cheap labor would have been a cruelty, a neglect most abhorrent to a fair and generous people, a shame to the Union of States. To leave it thus meant a destruction of its great industry, its relegation to bankruptcy. The Republican party has no such heart; the business welfare of our common country does not require it. A bounty was substituted for the duty which had been the protection.

But I need not defend Louisiana. She has able statesmen to take care of her interests. The interest is growing up in California to which I will soon refer. The payment of the bounty has become a question of controversy and opposition throughout the United States and by people of all parties and classes. The bounty on sugar is not the only one that has been granted by the Government nor denounced by the people. Have these resulted beneficially? Before the Republican party came into existence bounties were paid for public improvements. The great national pike of the time of Jackson was a national work for the benefit of a limited section of the States through which it passed, and no one ever begrudged the bounty by which it was constructed. The granting of public lands to aid in the construction of the Illinois Central Railroad, and the Michigan and Illinois Canal were bounties given by Democratic statesmen. All improvements to rivers and harbors are but bounties to localities, perhaps large or small, aggregating for the general good and national glory.

The Policy of the Bounty.

But they are made where localities were unable to protect themselves or make the improvements necessary for progress. The Western pioneers demanded that bounties in land and money be given for the construction of railroads threading the wilderness and reaching the Pacific. They were granted, and if in some respects without wise restrictions, certainly for the general good, and resulting in the creation of great States and developing untold wealth where otherwise were desert wastes traversable only by severest toil, dire suffering, and constant warfare, occupied by wild animals and savage tribes. Will anyone at this day controvert the beneficence of the bounties which have resulted so grandly in the cause of civilization and our country's development? I am reminded by seeing my friend from Maine [Mr. FRYE] that when he and I were boys the Government paid a bounty to those who engaged in cod fishing and went out and remained so many we ks or months fishing. That was done, too, under a Democratic administration.

Mr. FRYE. The Senator from California might go one word further and say that the fishermen who received the bounty afterwards paid it all back by helping us to beat Great Britain in 1812.

Mr. PERKINS. It therefore proved a most excellent investment. It was seed cast upon the water that returned ten, aye a hundred fold, to benefit the people as a whole who had given this small bounty.

The Sugar Industry in California.

But more particularly will I refer to the development of the sugar industry in my own State. Under tariff protection and with the McKinley bounty, mills for the manufacture of sugar from beets have been established with the prospect of eminent success. There are now three beet-sugar mills of large capacity in California. There is soil and room for a hundred more. It would require a thousand such as the largest in existence to supply the present consumption in the United States, and with the increased consumption the increased population, wealth, and varied uses will give, not many years will pass before double the number will be required.

The consumption in 1860 was at the rate of 56 pounds per capita. In England the consumption was at the rate of 67 pounds per capita; in other countries less. As it becomes cheaper, as our people advance in prosperity and as our fruit interests develop the consumption will increase in a greater ratio. The product of the world exceeds 5,000,000 tons per annum. About 60 per cent of the whole is made from beets. This sugar is, chemically, the same as cane sugar, and no one from its appearance or use can distinguish a difference. The product of sugar from beets per acre in America is estimated at from 1½ to 2 tons, demanding 2,000,000 acres of favored land to supply the present home demand.

The Benefits of the Sugar Mill.

The farmer and the community surrounding the sugar mill, the men who perform the labor, those who furnish the supplies to the mill, and those who supply the operatives, the transportation people, and all far-reaching are benefited. A mill disburses from $150,000 to $500,000 annually in the community where it is located. This builds up many happy and comfortable homes. Every mill means a prosperous village with its families, churches, schools, shops, manufactures, and well-paid labor with money that would otherwise go to some foreign country, leaving the land unoccupied or engaged in the production of something of which we have already an oversupply. The mill, representing a half million investment, is but a small part of the value it has created in its surroundings. Multiply this by a thousand, the number of mills and communities necessary to supply the United States, and we have an inconceivable valuation as the result of the judicious encouragement of this industry.

In the discussion of this bill some opponents of protection have asserted that our country profits most when its imports exceed the value of its exports. I would ask if anyone can contend that if we send abroad $100,000,000 for sugar we profit more than if the same were disbursed in Louisiana, California, Texas, Utah, Nebraska, and other States where sugar is or may be manu- factured? To say that it would be more profitable is a palpable absurdity. One throws away, the other retains. To buy when we can produce is waste and ultimate exhaustion. A little bounty insures this production, a bounty which at present and for some years is but a few cents per capita of tho people of the United States, wherein a duty as before the McKinley bill was enacted would be 88 cents per capita. But the 88 cents paid by each man, woman, and child is not all the exactions upon the people from a commodity like sugar imported. Trusts and combinations of monopoly are now formed which would be impossible if the peo- ple throughout the United States were engaged in the manu- facture.

The Importance of the Bounty.

By free importation and the bounty repealed the sugar indus- try is destroyed. To destroy an industry that now bids so fair would be a national calamity, a crime against our people, a deg- radation of statesmanship.

I appeal to the Senate not to let this be done. This important industry has been built up in other countries by the wise states- men in granting aid. The great Napoleon saw the necessity of the home production of sugar when the harbors of France were blockaded by English fleets and his merchantmen harassed by English cruisers, and he it was who inaugurated the production of beet sugar. Perhaps our strength will forbid a blockade, but with a war against a strong foreign power we would feel much more at ease if we made our own sugar. European travelers ob- serve our neglect of the beet-sugar opportunity with astonish- ment. Prof. Anton Veith, director of the Agricultural College of Bohemia, publishing his observations of a tour in the United States some years ago, says:

The establishing of such an industry as the fabrication of sugar from beets exerts such a great influence upon a country that it deserves all the support of a great government.

During the past summer the German Government sent a num- ber of experts to this country with the special object of exam- ining American agriculture, and particularly the beet-sugar in- dustry. Prof. Alexander Herzfeldt, one of these commission- ers, said:

If the United States shall continue to protect the sugar industry so that the development that now seems assured by protection may not be dis- turbed, the American market will be lost to Germany and France.—*New York Tribune.*

This bill proposes with no former notification whatever, to absolutely repeal the bounty clause of existing law. The law of 1890, the McKinley act, promised and agreed that "On and after July 1, 1891, and until July 1, 1905" there should be paid to our domestic producers of sugar from 1¾ to 2 cents per pound, de- pending on its quality.

A Clear Case of Repudiation.

I do not like the idea of repudiation in any form, and I can never consent by my vote, and without my protest, that this Government shall ever be a party to it. It is a repudiation of the contract pure and simple to pass this bill as it stands. Sugar sells to-day so cheap that no one can afford to adulterate it, for the adulteration will cost more than pure sugar. Consumers pay for it from 5 to 5¼ cents, which is 2½ cents per pound cheaper than the price which prevailed before the bounty law was passed. It is clear to me that the repeal of this bounty, unless something is given in return, will not only kill our home industry, but will hand over the market to foreign sugar rivals.

Danger to the Beet Sugar Manufacturers.

The beet sugar manufacturers are held to-day for contracts made with farmers of beets, extending over this and next year, and this repeal will force them into bankruptcy by the heavy losses on their contracts. The McKinley act, especially that portion relating to the sugar bounty, was no ordinary tariff bill, subject to change from year to year, but an absolute, declared contract for a certain number of years, for fourteen years. Citizens of California had confidence in the promise, the contract of the Government, and invested millions in the beet industry and the establishment of mills to manufacture the sugar. It is as clear as the noonday sun that there is an inevitable loss if this bounty is repealed and nothing of an equivalent offered in its place.

Useful Minerals of California.

Of sulphur and salt, Alameda County, my home, alone producing over 45,000 tons of salt per year, and ferro-manganese and many other minerals and their manufactures either on or to be put on the free list these arguments would be repeated. All these useful minerals abound in and make up the wealth of California and the great plateau of the West—a region of unbounded mineral resources, a region in the heart of our country supplying that which is demanded in the commerce and manufactures of all countries from the lowest barbarism to the highest civilization, which gives wealth to the producer, employment through countless industries, strength to the Government, and in turn affords a market to manufactures and products of every grade.

Not Entirely a Local Question.

By a strange fatality of most unfortunate experimental financiering, of which our country was not the originator nor wholly responsible, this great and important region has been made to suffer the loss of one of its principal resources, and now it may ask that other resources may be protected, that all may not be destroyed. While frequently referring to the products of my own State as subjects worthy of protection and feasible for purposes of revenue, I do not propose to make of the tariff an entirely local question; though good Democratic authority has asserted and maintained it was and is. But the products of California are so varied and so important to the commerce, the manufactures, and the comfort of the other States of the Union that all are worthy of special mention and the care of the Government.

That the claim that by a skillful levying of duties the foreign producer or manufacturer is made to pay a part of our revenue is not a fantasy, a dream, or a delusion, it is but necessary to refer to the case presented by the Bermuda farmers, now become so well known in the Ways and Means investigation. Another brought to my attention, of a manufacturer in New York of dye-

stuffs, of which he exported large quantities to Germany. That
country, seeing another opportunity for revenue and protection, imposed a specific duty upon the goods. Every particle of
this duty was, and is to this day, paid by the New York manufacturer, as he could not add it to the price of his dyestuffs in
the German market. This fact, however, is so evident in the
business affairs of our own country that it is unnecessary to argue
it to reasoning and observing people. Duties laid thus skill-
fully have that effect, affording the easiest paid revenue and ut
the same time protecting home industries, and such is the Mc-
Kinley tariff bill, which ought, perhaps with some modifications,
to remain the law of our land for a long time to come.

The Wool Industry.

The production and manufacture of wool is one of the great industries of California as well as of the United States: California
having produced more wool in 1893—26,803,414 pounds—than any
other State in the United States, and being the third State in
the matter of the number of sheep, having in 1893, 4,124,376
sheep, Ohio being the first with 4,378,725, and Texas second with
4,334,551 sheep. In fact, it is one of the great industries of the
world and has through a long series of years in all the enlightened governments by the world been a subject of the most pro-
found consideration of kings, statesmen, and the people. Spain
protected its merino sheep by inhibiting t eir exportation under
severe penalties. Australia encourages sheep-raising by grants
of vast ranges at nominal rates, as do the South American States
and other countries.

The policy of all has been that of protection and encouragement. Only in America has there arisen the strange and fac-
tional opposition to the industry. This fierce, unrelenting, and
unreasoning opposition is one of the relics of the sectional dis-
putes and interests of a past generation. Cotton against wool;
the export of one and the free importation of the manufacture of
the other, permeates with baleful influence the politics of the
present day. Complaint is made that the farmer is called upon
to bear the burdens of taxation with less assistance from Government than any other vocation. This complaint should be
heard and the grounds for it removed as far as possible.

Agriculture, the Basis of all Industries.

Agriculture has been honored through all history, and is the
basis of all industries. From the farm comes the sustenance of
all, and from the fields come the stalwart sons for the country's
defense and for its development. America, with its broad area
and fertile soil, depends more than any other country upon its
farmers, and every fostering care within the power of government should be extended in their behalf. Theirs is a life of toil,
where monopolies are impossible and guilds are of no avail.
Their burden of taxation is unavoidable, but theories threaten
them with more, to the extinction of their independence. Truly
has the poet said:

Ill fares the land, to hastening ills a prey,
Where wealth accumulates, and men decay.
Princes and lords may flourish or may fade—
A breath can make them, as a breath has made;
But a bold peasantry, their country's pride,
When once destroy'd, can never be supplied.

Let our theory be to lighten the burdens where possible and to assist where the opportunity offers. In almost every turn of our legislation the opportunity offers. Let us improve it.

The Record of the Republican Party.

The record of the Republican party may be proudly cited in its legislation for the farmer; in its investigations and publications for the farmer's benefit; in the homestead and liberal land laws; in the establishing of a Department of Agriculture and of experimental stations; in its grants to agricultural colleges and universities; in its aid to lines of transportation; in its systems of internal improvements, and countless other ways.

Let us for a moment consider how we may farther extend that aid. Take the single industry of woolgrowing. The aggregate is made of singles. A tariff on wool is both protective and revenue. In 1892 the value of raw wool imported was $17,697,037.50, on which a revenue was collected of $7,799,085.63, under a tariff of 11, 12, and 15 cents per pound. By the present bill this revenue, so urgently required at the present time, of eight millions of dollars is thrown away or put on the onerous burden of internal revenue, income tax or issue of interest-bearing bonds, and the incidental protection that was given is obliterated.

The Statistics of the Wool Industry.

The Agricultural Report of 1893 shows there are 47,273,553 sheep in the United States, in 47 States and Territories. Massachusetts, Rhode Island, Connecticut, New Jersey, Delaware, and South Carolina are the only States having each less than 100,000. Ohio, Texas, and California hold the largest number, each having over 4,000,000. Texas and California are of very large area, so their proportion of sheep to acreage is far below many of the other States and Territories. The production of wool in the United States in 1892 was 294,000,000 pounds, and the amount imported in the year ending June 30, 1893, was 172,435,838 pounds. The production and the importation have increased steadily for a series of years.

The wool production of the world is estimated at 2,456,773,600 pounds annually. The largest producers are Australia, Argentina, United States, and Russia, in the order mentioned. We are thus shown the countries with which we must compete. They are countries of vast areas of cheap grazing lands, against which the farmers of the United States should not be called upon to compete on equal terms, particularly when we require the revenue the incidental protection gives.

But we are told that the tariff imposes a grievous burden on the farmer in his purchases of clothing, and that the tariff has made it possible to force upon the people cloth of a poor quality. While this is known by all intelligent people to be untrue and is easily contradicted, we may take some evidence given before the Ways and Means Committee. Mr. Latzko, the Australian commissioner to the World's Fair, testified that—

The American woolen goods had no superior in any part of the world; there is nothing manufactured from wool that can not be as well made in this country as anywhere else.

The difference between free raw material in London and protected raw material under the McKinley law for a fine dress suit is just 90 cents.

The difference in the cost of material for a workingman's suit in this country and Great Britain is just 75 cents. All the other difference in the cost of the suit is the difference in the wages paid to laborers.

The wool industry of this country ranks seventh largest of the agricultural interests, and amounts to $66,000,000 annually. But take the tariff from wool, let that great interest die out, and the cloth for the workingman's suit may cost 75 cents less and the country will have to send $66,000,000 in gold or its equivalent abroad to pay for the wool. You will say this industry will not entirely die out. Probably not. Sheep for mutton will be grown, and then, as the wool will be of little value a high price will necessarily be charged for mutton, which will raise it to the class of luxuries, and the poor man who attempts to eat mutton will find his annual expenditures therefor a hundred times greater under free wool than under protected wool.

High Priced Mutton a Result.

This I know will be the result in my State, where good mutton is the meat of those exercising economy. We know how anxious are Argentina and Australia that we should admit their wool and pelts free of duty. Then they assert they will drive the American producer from the market in all the products except the fresh meat, and this will come later under the cold-storage system. This plainly shows what we must avoid. To be forewarned is to be forearmed.

We are here to legislate for American good and not for the good of a foreign country, however friendly we may feel for that country. The questions arising in adjusting the tariff are national and for the nation are purely selfish. I can not close this branch of the subject without referring to the petitions which I have received and presented in this body. This special one claims to be signed by over 10,000 woolgrowers of California:

To the honorable members of the Fifty-third Congress of the United States:

Whereas, as a result of a general belief that the tariff on woolen goods will be reduced and wool put on the free list, the price of wool is now below the production; and

Whereas we believe that if wool is put on the free list, and the tariff on woolen goods materially reduced, the price of wool will be still lower; and

Whereas we can not afford to raise wool in competition with free wool raised in countries like Australia, where the woolgrower rents land from the Government at a less rental than we pay in taxes on our land, and receives Government aid and encouragement; and

Whereas the lands of these United States are well suited to the raising of sheep, provided we can get a fair price for our wool and mutton; and

Whereas we believe that it is to the best interests of this country to prevent the slaughter of a large proportion of the sheep of this country, which will be the certain result of a further reduction in the price of wool:

We, the undersigned, farmers and woolgrowers, irrespective of party, do hereby petition and beg that your honorable body will make no change in the present tariff affecting the wool and woolen schedule now in force.

The Problems of the Day.

We are indeed confronted with the strange problem of an overcrowded people—a problem which the fathers of the Republic never dreamed would come so soon. To this may be added the marvelous devices of invention in the direction of labor-saving machinery. Men were never so cheap nor muscle so superfluous in the work of the world as now. The star of empire has moved westward until the tide of population has met the confines of the Pacific. We find unemployed men everywhere. Everywhere enforced idleness and suffering. It was not so in the early history of the Republic. It was not so before the attempt to depreciate the intrinsic value of one-half of our circulating medium. And, indeed, it was not so before the threatened blight of free trade fell upon the country.

Government by the people is only enduring where the best interests of the people are promoted. There can be no class distinctions or favoritisms in the collection or disbursing of revenue, and no system for raising revenue has ever equaled in unobjectionable simplicity that of our present tariff. Its greatest virtue consists in the fact that it is American. When we seek to foster other nations at the expense of our own, or so manage our own affairs as best to favor the industrial interests of other countries looking to a market among us, we are feeding a dry rot that means the ultimate decay of our institutions. It is not pleasant to take this view of the case, but it is the true view nevertheless. We have not yet reached that halcyon time when the consideration of a common humanity is the basis principle of the upbuilding of nations. The millenium is a long way off yet. Our idle mines and factories, our multitudes of hungry and unemployed operatives, our depreciated currency, all voice this fact as never before in the history of this country.

The General Depression of Trade.

The present Administration assumed the control of the country the 4th of March, 1893. During the seven months following, as shown by Bradstreet, the falling off in the business of the clearing house amounted to the vast sum of nearly $5,000,000,-000, and it has kept up at that fearful rate ever since. This stupendous deficit represents the country's value of trade. Twelve billions of dollars less money circulated in the ordinary channels of trade and commerce, in wages, in the manufacture of goods. in the employment of labor. And all this under the proposed free-trade policy, or, as they like to be called, tariff reformers, of the present Administration, in the brief period of twelve months. Indeed, the nation stands appalled before the peril that threatens. Cities swarming with the unemployed, mines and factories closed, an army of unemployed marching from the west and north toward Washington—no such general depression of the ordinary industries of the country finds a parallel in our history.

The Policy of England, Not American.

Carry out the policy of England concerning this country; make it contributory to her greatness regardless of the effect upon our people and industries, and what becomes of the magic attraction of our flag, what will there be left to inspire patriotism, or make this land the hope of the oppressed? Divest this country of its policy of protection and there will be nothing in its citizenship to call forth the admiration of mankind. Its labor must degenerate to a level with that of the Old World's, with which it will be brought in immediate competition. We shall have squandered our birthright to placate other nations by placing our standards of labor on a level with their own. We should blush for the American party (and all parties in this great country ought to be American) that has no higher conception of the nation's needs. This ought to be the richest country in the world; taxes should be the lowest. Labor on a higher standard and better paid, its products bring the greatest satisfaction. All of which it would be and do but for the Anglomania that has turned the heads of a large portion of our people, especially of one of our great political parties.

Let American Patriotism Animate Us.

Every avenue to wealth and fame is open to the humblest boy in this land. Yonder little schoolhouse on the hill is the stepping stone to the highest niche in the temple of fame in this land. It is true American manhood that makes the man in this glorious land. I have traveled all over the world: I have been in every land, on every continent of this great globe; I have been in the frozen north, in the tropics, in the frozen south where the Southern Cross is seen like the Great Bear of the north pole; I have been in the islands of the Pacific, in the islands of the Indian Ocean: but nowhere on God s universe have I ever seen a land like this. I have, as the patriarch of old, approached the temple to pay homage to the Unknown, as I saw the Star Spangled Banner floating over the consul's house in the north of Europe or in Southern Africa felt as Moses did when he stood near the burning bush, that I stood upon sacred ground, and I involuntarily removed my hat from my head and thanked God that I was an American. Let our votes and our actions be in harmony and accord with this true American spirit of patriotism that should animate our hearts.

An Era of Snobs and Snobbishness.

There is nothing genuine with some so-called Americans in their estimation that does not wear a foreign stamp. They furnish their homes with the products and works of foreign manufacture, they wear foreign-made clothing, eat foreign viands, drink foreign wine, and smoke foreign cigars. This is the class of people that I like to give the full benefit of a tariff intended to protect American industries. Any abridgment of our protective policy is a step in the direction of national decay, and so the intelligent thought of the people declare at the ballot box in the elections in Ohio, Massachusetts, Iowa, New Jersey, and Rhode Island. Year after year, much of the time of Congress is devoted to the assailing on the one hand and defending on the other this last vestige of American policy. But for the last quarter of a century the people have had no fears of the result, as they knew that the party that would be safely trusted in the matter held sway in one or the other branch of the National Legislature.

A Contrast of Histories.

Take the history of our Government from the first and the policy of England towards us has been strangely varied. When we were weak she was strong and at the same time aggressively protective. This was prior to the adoption of the "free-trade policy of 1846, forced upon the country in response to the demands of the South, because of the predominating influence of the North, the result of free labor" over that portion of the country where chattel slavery prevailed. England did not then feel assured that she could bear the competition of continental nations, and, as is well known to anyone familiar with our history, she manufactured for herself and for her network of colonies reaching around the globe. Into those colonies no other nation could carry anything. There was no scale of duty upon which other nations could enter the colonial ports. What the colonies needed outside of British product could be furnished to them only in British ships. This was, then, her idea of protection—the protection her great Premier Gladstone has declared to be immoral. But it was not protection; it was prohibition, absolute and remorseless. And it was continued even to the day when Mr. Gladstone entered upon his long and splendid career in Parliament.

The Dignity of Labor.

The dignity of labor should ever be uppermost in the American mind, and the only way for us to dignify it is to bar out from competition the servile and cheap labor of those countries where a man's worth and social standing depend not upon his own merits, but upon some advantageous circumstance ceded to or stolen by some favorite ancestor. A protective tariff should be the last surrender of this Republic to kingcraft. It is the guerdon of our greatness, the bulwark of our manhood. Every attempt to fasten free trade upon this country has been followed by financial depression and disaster. This last attempt brings such hardship to our industrial interests as has never before blighted this fair land. If we are wise we ought to learn something in this school of experience. We should guard with jealous care this last feature that distinguishes us from the effete institutions of the Old World.

The American artisan and laborer have long held a distinguished place in this country. There is none above them; but how long will it be thus, without protection? Compare their surroundings with those of this class in other countries. Squalor and poverty on the one hand—plenty and often luxury on the other. So long as labor is not crowned king, as it is metaphorically with us, in countries depending on us for a market, we can never allow our laboring men the humiliation of competition.

Cheap Wares Not All that is Needed.

We have by legislation wisely, in my opinion, excluded immigration of the pauper and contract laborer from Europe, and the servile Chinese laborer from Asia, but by the proposed legislation we are to permit the product of the Chinese factories in China, where labor is but 10 cents a day, to come into our country and sell in competition with the products of American workshops that are operated by American workmen. To do this is to shock the sensibilities of every patriotic citizen. Cheap wares are not the only things we need. The farmer needs a market for his product at good prices and he can have such a market only when the mechanic, the miner, the factory hands find ready employment at good wages. Rightly says the Inter-Ocean—

The Republican tariff made the home of American workmen a home of plenty. He lived and enjoyed the luxuries of the rich in the older lands. The Democratic policy in its very promise, and before its reality could be experienced, has brought distrust and want and suffering. It is that and nothing else. The talk about silver producing the hard times was simply a Democratic blind.

Free trade is only desirable of those things we can not produce or manufacture, and even then the necessities of our revenue may require a moderate tariff which our people will never begrudge. We are contending for one of the basic principles of the Republic without which our bond of union becomes a rope of sand. To the hundreds of thousands unemployed men in the different States of the Union it is that already, with the mere shadow of "free trade" hanging over us.

Should be Revised by Friends of the System.

I am not arguing against the possible necessity for a revision of the tariff, but such a revision can never be intrusted to the Democratic party as now organized. The revision should be made, if at all, by those in sympathy with the protection of American labor and American industries, and then with a view to increasing and not diminishing the revenue. The measure of the necessity for a protective tariff may be wisely gauged by the number of unemployed men in the nation. By the status of manufacturing industries—by the demand for our agricultural products. These are the reasons of our needs for raising of the revenues necessary for the expenses of the Government. The amount required is about $500,000,000 annually. To raise the largest part of this vast sum by any other method than that of a tax on imports would be the sublimest piece of folly ever imposed upon a nation.

Several bills have been introduced looking to the creation of a non-partisan commission for the purpose of thoroughly revising the tariff duties based upon the difference in the cost of American and foreign labor, thereby promoting and encouraging our own domestic industries, and at the same time elevating and advancing the dignity of American labor. In the establishment of two of our greatest industries, namely, the manufacture of Bessemer steel and plate glass, it was accomplished only after repeated failures and the expenditure of vast sums of money, and then only by a most liberal encouragement on the part of the Government, without which success would have been impossible. In all American manufactures the higher wages of American mechanics is the chief factor in, as well as the pride and glory of our institutions. It is our glory that our artisans may live in competence, educate their families and surround themselves with comforts that belong only to the rich in the older countries.

How our Fathers Viewed the Question.

It may not be amiss in this connection to present some of the opinions of the fathers on this momentous subject. When the Colonies obtained their political independence they naturally wished to establish their industrial independence also. That great Scotchman, Alexander Hamilton, first struck the keynote of the second struggle when, as Secretary of the Treasury, December 5, 1791, he said:

This idea of an extensive domestic marke t for the surplus product of the soil is of the first consequence. It is of all things that which most effectually conduces to a flourishing state of agriculture. To secure such a market there is no other expedient than to promote manufacturing establishments. It is the interest of a community, with a view to eventual and foreign economy, to encourage the growth of manufactures. In a national view, a temporary enhancement of price must always be well compensated by a prominent reduction of it.

American statesmen have followed in similar strains. Thus Washington's last annual address, December 7, 1796, says:

Congress have repeatedly and not without success, directed their attention to the encouragement of manufacturers. The object is of too much consequence not to secure a continuance of their efforts in every way which shall appear eligible.

President Madison, in his special message of May 23, 1809, says:

It will be worthy at the same time, of their just and provident care, to make such further alterations in the laws as will more especially protect and foster the several branches of manufacture which have been recently instituted as extended by the laudable exertion of our citizens.

Thomas Jefferson, in a letter to Benjamin Austin, of Boston, 1816, says:

To be independent for the comforts of life, we must fabricate them ourselves; we must place our manufacturers by the side of the agriculturists. Experience has taught me that manufactures are now as necessary to our independence as to our comfort.

President Monroe, in his first inaugural address, March 5, 1817, says:

Our manufactures will likewise require the systematic and fostering care of the Government. Possessing as we do all the raw materials, the fruit of our own soil and industry, we ought not to depend, in the degree we have done, on supplies on other countries. While we are thus dependent, these sudden events of war, unsought and unexpected, can not fail to plunge us into the most serious difficulties.

President Jackson, August, 26, 1824, says:

Heaven has smiled upon and gave us liberty and independence. The same Providence has blessed us with the means of national dependence and national defense. If we omit or refuse to use the gifts which He has extended to us, we deserve not the continuance of His blessing. He has filled our mountains and plains with minerals and given us a climate and soil for the growing of hemp and wool. These being the great materials of our national defense, they ought to have extended to them adequate and fair protection, that our manufacturers and laborers may be placed in a fair competition with those of Europe, and that we may have within our country a supply of these leading articles so essential to war.

The cause of that disparity of conditions having been removed, there is no longer any good reason why the people of the South should not favor protection, a condition of things most essential to her prosperity. Most serious disturbances of our business affairs come of any interference with the tariff. The man who has erected his mills and his factories under protection of his products, with the withdrawal of that protection, is most seriously disturbed, if not ruined.

The Act of the Administration.

It seems to be more a determination on the part of the Administration to carry out an idea, erroneous as we may believe it to be, than any demand of the people or any especial need or emergency of the times. If we think the voice of the people can be stilled on these great questions affecting the policy of the nation, we mistake the nature of this Government. It needs no prophet to predict that the people have had quite enough of this partisan tampering with the tariff. You will see what they will say in the next elections, when the question comes home to them as it will. And the political party that would retain or obtain a lease of power in the future would do well to heed this voice, the source of all power in this nation.

The condition of affairs in this country is vastly different from what it was a quarter of a century or more ago. The discontented and unsettled classes, of which the number is steadily increasing, have no longer new and virgin territory to occupy when they become dissatisfied with the older communities. The time has come when in the order of things we must have a fixed national policy upon all questions affecting the stability of the Government.

We can endure less foolishness than formerly. The people can stand less nonsense in the shape of unwise laws than when there was less suffering and idleness among them. These freaks of legislation, if we may so call them, should be forced upon the country only in time of great prosperity. Our free trade "or tariff for a deficiency" friends seem to be oblivious to this fact.

Why we Oppose the Bill.

We oppose this bill because it works a serious diminution of our revenue on foreign imports, because the people do not want it, because it would cripple our industries, and because the present condition of the country is most unfavorable for any such innovation. We should beware at such times of any disturbing acts of legislation which tend to unsettle the quiet of the country. We should bear in mind that under the existing tariff which this bill proposes to disturb, there is an estimated deficiency made by the Secretary of the Treasury of $78,000,000 for the current year. And in the revenue bill proposed by this new schedule, it is proposed to discard $76,000,000 from the present tariff and impose a new form of internal and direct taxation upon our people to make up for this deficiency.

An Unwise and Reckless Proposition.

A proposition more unwise in these unsettled times could not well be devised; and strange it seems to me, that a party that one would naturally expect to see laying the foundation of future power—a party seeking to hold itself in sympathy and touch with the people—should in this reckless way throw away all chances to future promotion or ascendency. With the motto of Dante, written above the entrance to his inferno, "Abandon hope all ye who enter here," it may well be said of all those misguided statesmen who have entered into this conspiracy against protection, abandon all hope for preferment of the people ye unwise ones who seek to overthrow the main pillar of our institutions. If I did not prefer the prosperity of my country to that of party, I would withhold this warning cry and let them rush to certain disaster.

"A tariff for revenue only!" exclaim the champions of free trade. Exactly, say the people, but give us enough tariff for enough revenue, which means no reduction of the present rates, but on the other hand such advance upon many articles as may at least work an increase equal to the present deficiency. I want to emphasize the matter I have already referred to concerning an American policy in customs and finance. We have a territory as great as that of all Europe and a population which a few years hence will excel that of all English-speaking countries combined. And yet we have no policy of our own—no financial policy that is not made for us in the financial centers of the Old World. Our definition of money is vague, indefinite, and intensely English. With an immense territory and population we seem to be denied a distinctive policy of finance of our own. We must first ascertain what is wanted of us and then quietly and submissively yield up our own manhood to the keeping of others. This should never be submitted to by those who prefer the American Republic and her institutions as superior to those of any other lands.

The Fruit, Wine, and Nut Industries.

The proposed new tariff bill especially affects the great fruit, wine, and nut industries of California, and will ruin them if it becomes a law in the proposed form. These industries are wonderful in view of the fact that it is in the memory of the man of middle age in this country when they were started. There is scarcely a city or town in the country where California fruits, nuts, and wine can not be purchased. While the trade is enormous there has not been as much profit in it as is generally understood. There are many reasons for this, but the principal one is the difficulty and expense in securing the market for the goods and cost of transportation to the consumer. The fruits, nuts, and wine have had to fight every foot for the position they now occupy in the markets of the United States, for the foreign productions only yielded because they were forced to, and for the additional reason that the fruits, nuts, and wines of California have not only undersold them, but because, also, they—the home productions—have been of better quality.

If it is pardonable at any time to introduce in a speech of this character statistics and tables showing the growth and quantity of California's productions in this line, this would be a case; but I forbear, for I am thoroughly convinced that it needs no such array to show that they are appreciated and are in demand. Later on, however, when this bill is under consideration by paragraphs, I may offer the Senate some statistics on the question. These great industries grew because they were given protection by our laws, and though they may not be classed as infant industries, they are still comparatively new, and will for some years yet need a fair and legitimate protection in their competition with the Old World. A severe blow has been given them by this bill, and unless it is amended an irreparable damage will be done.

The Importance and Necessity of Protection.

California sent out last year 2,500 carloads of 12 tons each of raisins, and this year will send out 3,700 carloads. Add to these the thousands of carloads of oranges, peaches, apricots, pears, figs, plums, prunes, etc., fresh, preserved, canned, and dried, and one can in a small degree realize the importance of the industry, and I hope realize the necessity of protection. California to-day has 12,000 acres of almonds, and is probably the only State in the Union interested as a grower. Her forests of walnut trees are also threatened by the reduction of the duty. Even worse than the reduction is the doing away with the specific duty and the change to the ad valorem, for there is hardly any calculating the injury the change will make. The duties levied by the present law are none too high, while those proposed by this bill if not changed will almost bring about an abandonment of the industry.

Wine Makers Specially Injured.

In regard to the wine industry, what can I add, in opposition to the passage of this bill? It is a bill that is wrong in so many directions that it would take days to enumerate them. In no one, however, does it do more harm than it does to the wine-maker of California, or indeed to the wine-maker of other States, when it abolishes specific and establishes ad valorem duties. This feature was introduced at the very last moment, and without question through the efforts of importers of foreign wines, or possibly of the producers of European wines, more particularly of those of France. The bill reads that the duty on still wines in casks shall remain as it has been, viz, 50 cents per gallon, but that it shall not exceed 100 per cent ad valorem.

This, on the face, appears to be a very large protection, but when you consider that the production of wines in Europe, especially this year, has been very great—thus in France fully 1,300,000,000 gallons against an average crop of barely half of this, and Italy a crop of possibly six to eight hundred million—you will well understand that the price of such wines in Europe will be very low, and I have no doubt that the cheaper grades will not average above 10 cents per gallon there. This means, according to the wording of the bill, a duty of 10 cents per gallon upon such wines, a figure considerably lower than was ever asked on the part of importers here. Besides this, there are many parts of France and Germany where wines are artificially manufactured—thus in Cette, France, and in Hamburg, Germany—and as the basis of such wines is potato or grain spirits, which pay no tax, as they are intended for wines for export, and which spirits cost possibly 6 to 8 cents per gallon, one can well imagine how cheap they can produce so-called wines, particularly as the balance that they add is in the form of chemicals.

An Era of Cheap and Fraudulent Wines.

It must be understood that it is difficult to appraise the value of wines, for they can not be judged as other manufactured articles are, for the reason that even the best judges differ as to the value of goods, and as many of the goods are shipped by the producers, the latter can put an arbitrary value upon their wine, as they may possibly figure only cost of production and interest upon their investment. This would result in the shipment of altogether or to a great extent low-priced wines.

In this connection I have received a letter from Mr. John T. Doyle, president of the viticultural commission of California, himself a prominent leading Democrat, in which, discussing this bill, he says, and as he states the case better and stronger than I can, I quote from it:

The 50 cents per gallon is in no sense a protective duty. It was in force long before the McKinley bill was thought of, and I am not aware of any suggestion to change it in past years. The fact that the wine raised in this State does not average the producer 15 cents per gallon is conclusive evidence of the nonproductive character of the duty. Wine is ordinarily an article of luxury, and a most proper subject for a revenue duty. It is, also, an article so difficult to fix a true value on by any external test that any but a specific duty would be quite out of place. An ad valorem duty on wine is an absurdity. * * *

But there is a stuff called wine, which is made for exportation in France and Italy in enormous quantities, which should not be admitted to importation here on any terms. It is often filthy and nauseous in its mode of manufacture, and is really unfit for human consumption. A duty of 50 cents excludes it, for under no circumstances could it sell for so much; but I doubt if 100 or even 200 per cent ad valorem would, for it can probably be invoiced at 5 cents per gallon, or even less. The best of it is made by taking pomace after it has yielded all its wine to the press, adding glucose and water, and allowing it to ferment again.

The pomace gives the color and something of the flavor of wine, the glucose yields the necessary alcohol, which, if need be, is supplemented by German potato whisky, the most noxious of all the alcohols known to chemistry, and which is now finding its way all over the South of Europe as an ingredient of counterfeit wines and liquors. The pomace is thus used over and over again. The invasion of the French vineyards by the phyloxera led to the introduction of this counterfeit wine industry some years ago to supply the export trade of the country and it has since attained an enormous proportion.

* * * * * * *

We do not ask for any protection on wine, a duty that will give such revenue as is fairly collectible from such a luxury is all we need. But the public has a right to expect the Democratic party not to open the door, for the first time, to the importation of vicious and poisonous beverages under the pretense of freedom of trade. Free trade should at least be confined to honest commodities.

Other Industries Injuriously Affected.

There are besides those I have referred to many other interests of California affected injuriously by the various provisions of this bill. The reduction of duty upon lumber, rice, freestone, sandstone, onyx, lime, hops, beans, chicory, twine and cordage, burlaps, jute and bagging, and live stock will prostrate those industries as at present conducted. The struggling factories engaged in the manufacture of cotton, wool, rope, and jute can only continue by a corresponding reduction of wages to their employés. The placing of machinery for vessels on the free list will, I am afraid, result in closing several of the ship-building machine shops on the Pacific coast. They have been built up by the patient industry, pluck, and enterprise of our California mechanics. That they can do work to favorably compare with any country in the world, I have but to mention the United States ships Charleston, San Francisco, Oregon, Olympia, Monterey, and other steamships built by our mechanics of California.

But they can not continue to pay the same wages and compete with workmen on the Clyde who will manufacture and send machinery there at a nominal freight in ships that come to load wheat, and must have ballast on their outward trip to California. But I find that I have already occupied more of the time and attention of the Senate than I should at this time. I shall, however, claim the privilege when the bill is under discussion by schedules and paragraphs to offer amendments and to point out, discuss, and show to the Senate how the people of the State I have the honor in part to represent on this floor, will be injured if the bill becomes a law without very radical improvement.

We should maintain the integrity of the Republic in its dearest rights and usages, and should aim to uphold a higher order of manhood among our laboring classes than belongs to any monarchy on the face of the globe. God pity this land when a man's title to true nobility shall not depend solely upon his personal worth and merit; where the measure of his greatness hangs upon the empty bauble of a title conferred upon some worthless ancestor. There can be no heraldy of merit founded upon superior skill or genius in the great world of use. And herein should ever consist our superiority over the nations of the earth. When we foolishly surrender this boon this great Republic will surely fade from the nations of the earth.

The Question of Trusts and Coöperation.

I am not one of those who feel that they are called upon at all times and in all cases to denounce trusts, combinations, coöperative, or corporative investments. Many combinations produce more beneficial results than otherwise, and are in the interests of the people. There are unlawful trusts, however, which do harm and which menace legitimate interests in every direction. These should and can be regulated by law, State and national, and I stand ready to take my share of the responsibility in pass-

ing such laws, for I am convinced that such determined reme-
dial agents are necessary. I would crush out the trusts and
combinations which oppress as I would encourage and foster
those which are organized for beneficial purposes.

I am a thorough believer in "profit-sharing" enterprises—
coöperation and coöperative effort—for many good things can
be done by this means which are not possible by private capital
or private enterprise alone. Trusts when organized for the
public good should have proper encouragement, but when they
have reached the point where they, by aggregated capital and
combination of interests, attempt to, or influence, legislation,
either State or national, they should be removed and dispersed.

In explanation of a trust that has my unqualified indorsement,
I instance the case of the raisin men of five counties in California, Fresno, Tulare, Madera, Kings, and Kern Counties, which
have agreed that all raisins are to go into the hands of the or-
ganization to be sold, doing away entirely with middlemen. To
perfect this plan, they propose to raise a capital of say $200,000,
representing the same number of shares at $1 an acre, so that
there would be no need of resorting to commission houses for
advances. It is further proposed that each neighborhood or dis-
trict shall have a coöperative packing-house in order to reduce
the cost of preparing the goods for market. When a sale is
made the proceeds are divided pro rata among all who have
goods in the warehouse, so that no one could have any advantage over another. No one will be injured who does not join
the association. Consequently such a trust as this becomes a
public benefit.

The Iron and Coal Industry.

The question of free or dutiable iron and coal, as affecting the
interests of California, from a narrow point of view, may be debatable, but on a broad view of the suject we find we are in
touch with the coördinate welfare of our sister States of the
Union. We may ask if we can build up the highest prosperity
of our own, or any one State, while we neglect the interests of
others, or do we not profit most when others are prosperous?
California produces but little iron or coal. These commodities
are imported in large amounts, chiefly from foreign countries,
and in foreign ships, iron from England, Sweden, and Russia,
coal from Great Britain, Australia, and Vancouver Island.

California is the largest importer of coal of any State of the
Union, the amount being about 1,000,000 tons annually, and paying over $700,000 in duties to the National Treasury. Under
this bill the duties are very largely reduced and the consumer
expects them cheaper in our markets. But this expectation
will not be realized, as we generally find that an importer, as
well as anyone else, will charge all he can get for an article
whether he has paid duty on it or not, particularly when he, or
a syndicate, has the power of a monopoly.

Competition Keeps Down the Prices.

The production of coal on the Pacific coast, though small,
kept this monopoly down, or nearly down, and by the power of
competition, though limited, kept down the price to the consumer. But without the duty the American producers of coal
could not maintain themselves. It is doubted that the reduced
duty provided for in this bill will be sufficient to aid the Ameri-

can miners of coal to keep up their competition, though they will do so if they can, and the result may be that the trusts controlling the foreign coal will raise the price to consumers.

Mr. POWER. Will the Senator from California allow me?

Mr. PERKINS. Certainly.

Mr. POWER. Where do you get your coal used for the shipping interests?

Mr. PERKINS. As I was about to state, large quantities of it are brought from England, large quantities from Australia, and large quantities from British Columbia, with our own domestic product in Washington, Oregon, and California.

Mr. POWER. How does the coal produced in Washington and Oregon answer for the shipping interests?

Mr. PERKINS. For steam purposes?

Mr. POWER. For steam purposes.

Mr. PERKINS. The coal of California and Oregon has not been as good steam coal as that of Washington and British Columbia. However, the coal of the State of Washington, and I speak advisedly, has veins that compare favorably with any other steam coal upon the coast, its principal competitor being that of British Columbia or Vancouver Island.

Mr. POWER. Is the coal from the State of Washington as good as that from Vancouver Island?

Mr. PERKINS. I think in some of the mines it is quite equal to that of British Columbia.

Mr. POWER. The Government made a contract for the Bering Sea fleet in the last few weeks for coal from the British country, taking that coal in place of our product. I was called upon to look after that so far as some friends are concerned, and that is the reason why I asked the question. Why was that done?

Mr. PERKINS. The Senator from Montana calls my attention to the fact. I presume it is done to carry out the foreign policy of this Administration perhaps.

Mr. POWER. So I thought at the time.

Mr. PERKINS. I am somewhat a consumer of coal, being obliged to purchase from 5,000 to 10,000 tons monthly, and from an actual test in our experiments we find that the coal of the mines in the State of Washington called the Franklin mine, for steam purposes, is equal in its efficiency to that of any coal upon the Pacific coast, notwithstanding the Government in asking for bids or proposals for furnishing coal did not mention this mine, but advertised only for foreign coal.

Mr. POWER. That is what I understand.

Mr. PERKINS. Not being in accord with the present Administration I am unable to give my friend the information he desires.

Mr. ALDRICH. Will the Senator from California permit me?

Mr. PERKINS. Certainly.

Mr. ALDRICH. Does the Senator from California mean to be understood as saying that the bid of the Department excluded American coal?

Mr. PERKINS. I will not say that it excluded it, but it was not considered, I understand.

Mr. DAVIS. Has attention been called to the character of the Washington coal?

Mr. PERKINS. The case can hardly be otherwise, as the mines of the Washington coal have been worked for thirty years or more, and it is used continually by the steamships operating on the Pac fic coast. The company that I in part represent, engaged in operating steamships, consumes from 5,000 to 10,000 tons monthly; and I speak without reservation when I state that its effective use for steam purposes is equal to the coal of British Columbia or any other coal.

Mr. MITCHELL of Oregon. In addition to that, if the Senator will allow me, the special attention of the Secretary of the Navy was called to the fact that the Washington mines had been omitted, by a communication signed by several Senators, myself among the number.

Mr. DAVIS. What response was made to that communication?

Mr. MITCHELL of Oregon. The response was to the effect that under all the circumstances as far as they were advised they thought the British coal the best.

Mr. ALDRICH. If the Senator from California will further allow me, I beg to call the attention of my distinguished friend from West Virginia [Mr. FAULKNER] to the fact which has been stated by the Senator from Oregon, and to ask his influence with the Administration to see that domestic coals are properly treated hereafter.

Mr. FAULKNER. If the Senator from California will permit me, I am satisfied that the Administration which is now in power would certainly (if it was in accordance with an economic administration of the Department) much prefer the use of American coal to foreign coal, and I suppose it can only be by reason of misinformation in reference to the quality of the coal which could be furnished by those mines that they purchase at all the foreign coal to which the Senator from California has alluded.

Mr. PERKINS. I had not referred to this in my remarks; I tried not to be personal at all; and ordinarily I should defer to the judgment of the Senator from West Virginia; but I have some knowledge of coal, because the vessels which I am engaged in operating consume large quantities of coal and we know from actual test, not a theoretical experiment, but by burning 1,000 tons of coal from this mine and 1,000 tons of coal from the other mine, that the same speed of a vessel under similar circumstances is attained. That is the result.

Mr. MITCHELL of Oregon. I should like to ask a question right here. The Senator from California, as he states, and we all know, is a very large consumer of coal on the Pacific coast. That being so, of course one would naturally suppose that he would like to get the coal so used as cheaply as possible. Does the Senator think that by putting coal on the free list he in the course of a few years, if at all, would get his coal as cheaply as he does now?

Mr. PERKINS. I shall endeavor to demonstrate the fact, but my time is passing, and I wish to make a few remarks about the income tax. I shall have to file a special brief with my friend to show him that I am satisfied the consumer would not get his coal one cent less, judging the future by the past. Before our mines in Oregon, Washington, and California were developed (and we have a few of them in California) coal was always purchased from the ships to arrive, and the consumer was never benefited one cent thereby. But, parenthetically, speaking of the question of my friends from Montana and Oregon, it is t ue that our Government did not give our Oregonians and Washingtonians an opportunity of competing, yet I want to say a kind word for our friends in British Columbia. They are our neighbors, and they buy a great many goods from us in California. They are a very kind-hearted, hospitable people. They are an American people, who ought to be connected and allied with us by political bands.

To show how much more generous they are than our own Government, to one of the steamship companies that I can call to mind I think they have paid during the past twenty-five years a special mail subsidy for carrying the mails by steamer from San Francisco to Victoria, British Columbia, of from $5,000 to $10,000 a year; while our Government pays for carrying the mail about $1.50 a mail, I think. That is the policy. Therefore I feel very kindly toward our friends, and if they would unite themselves with the United States I should not object to purchasing our coal there altogether.

But since the Senators from Montana and Oregon have called attention to the discrimination against American coal, I am sure my friend from West Virginia, having a judicial mind, will say at once that there is some mistake and that he himself will volunteer to remedy this wrong, and in the next bid the coal of Washington and Oregon will be invited to compete.

Mr. FAULKNER. If the Senator will permit me, I have no doubt that after the Secretary of the Navy has read the very elaborate and satisfactory argument of the Senator from California on this subject and knows his ability to talk from personal knowledge of the quality of the coal there will be no difficulty whatever. I underst ind that this coal was excluded on the report of the officers who had tested it.

Mr. PERKINS. Since the question has been brought up I want to s iy in justice to the Department that while the Washington coal is just as effective and is equal for steam purposes, yet it is not quite as clean, and the officers prefer a harder coal that does not throw any cinders on the deck or upon their suits of clothing made of foreign wool. I think I can make it clear even to my friend from West Virginia that there should be a duty upon coal; but I wish to say that I have an interest in one mine and that I am interested in the management of a company which has investments in several coal mines; and while those who know me would hardly charge that it would influence me in my vote, yet as there are some evil-minded people who sometimes misconstrue a person's action, when the question of the coal duty is up for consideration I shall, with the permission of the Senate, refuse to vote upon it.

I do not believe it right for anyone to vote on any measure in which he has a direct interest, if it is ever so small; and yet to my satisfaction, and I think to the satisfaction of my friend from West Virginia, I can show that the duty should not be reduced from 75 cents to 40 cents a ton, and that after all the talk of "free coal" the people of the Pacific States would have "dear coal" as the results of their efforts. I am confident that the price will not be reduced, though the duty is, and the difference between existing duties and the reduced duties will go into the pockets of the foreign ship and mine owner. The trusts are powerful enough to do just as they did before when the duty was reduced to raise the price to make up the difference.

The Statistics of the Coal Question.

For the year 1892 the total output of the coal mines of the world was 539,000,000 tons. Of this the United States produced 179,000,000 tons, or nearly 33 per cent of the total. Of this product the United States exported from her Atlantic and lake ports—

	Tons.
Anthracite	851,000
Bituminous	1,645,000
Total	2,496,000

During the same year the United States imported—

	Tons.
Anthracite	65,058
Bituminous	1,143,000
Total	1,208,058

Leaving this general statement, and coming to the coal consumption of the State of California, the statistics show that she imported from all sources of supply during the years 1892 and 1893, viz:

	1892.	Per cent.	1893.	Per cent.
FOREIGN.	Tons.		Tons.	
British Columbia	554,600	35	588,527	40
Australia	314,230	20	202,017	13.5
Great Britain	235,560	15	170,078	11
Japan	4,220		7,758	.5
Total, dutiable and nondutiable	1,108,600	70	968,380	65
DOMESTIC.				
Washington	383,320	24	428,985	29.5
California and Oregon	66,150	4	63,460	4.5
Pennsylvania and Maryland	35,720	2	18,960	1
Total	485,190	30	511,405	35
Total importation	1,593,850	100	1,479,785	100

It may with safety be assumed that the 65,058 tons anthracite reported as coming into the United States were delivered at California ports. Deducting this from California's total importations of foreign coal will leave a balance of 1,043,000 tons of dutible bituminous coal brought to her ports, showing that only 100,000 tons foreign bituminous coal went into all other ports of the United States, and that of all the foreign coal imported during 1892, California received over 91 per cent.

It will thus be seen that California occupies a singular and unique position relative to the Government tax on fuel. This is because:

1. She has not within her borders any known deposits of coal suitable in quality for the general needs, and within reach of her centers of consumption.

2. She is the most populous of the sparsely settled Pacific coast States, and therefore offers the largest market west of the Rocky Mountains.

3. She is essentially an agricultural State, dependent upon distant markets for the sale of her products, and compelled largely to use ocean carriage for transportation. This fact attracts vessel tonnage, almost entirely foreign in nationality, and which coming from far distant points is chiefly laden with coal as inward cargoes.

If business policy, and not theories shall determine the right of government to protect by tariff those lines of business which need protection, shall get any consideration, that policy will be best which tends to encourage the development of resources to the profitable employment of capital and to the largest amount of work and rates of wages. What that amount of tariff, distinctly for protection, shall be, is the question for those who fix the rates, but unquestionably it should be no more and no less than is necessary to equalize the cost between the same grades of foreign and domestic material laid down at the seaboard ports.

California's Position Explained.

Respecting coal, California's position is different from that of every other State of the Union. Leaving out of the question any discussion that she may have interests requiring the help of sister States towards shaping the governmental policy for their protection, it is a fact that with her the farming element is the most important. The farmer pays the outward freight on his wheat because he gets for his product the difference between the foreign market rates and the freights by sailing ships. Therefore, whatever tends to increase the outward carrying tonnage, or what will lower the cost of wheat freights, is in the interest of the farmer.

Dismissing for a moment the reciprocal interests of California with her neighboring States, it is a fact that coal constitutes the largest volume of inbound freight; therefore, it is better for the farmer if the coal trade of the State shall be supplied from distant foreign ports, because—

1. The inward earnings enable the ships to carry the wheat outward at lower rates than would otherwise be possible.

2. Coal as cargo from distant foreign ports sends here an increased tonnage of wheat-carrying ships.

It therefore follows that the importation of coal from adjacent foreign ports is not in the interest of the farmer, because it is carried in British steamers and by other nonwheat-carrying vessels. The importation of coal from near foreign mines has two effects in California: It displaces the product of mines worked by American labor in adjoining States, and to the extent that it displaces the product of distant foreign mines, to just that extent does it lower the list of vessels that would otherwise be attracted to carry away California products.

It is entirely safe to say, and the statement will be borne out by unprejudiced experience, that the abolition of the present duty as proposed by the bill as it came here will shut the California market against the American coast mines, and lead to a further absorption of the coal tonnage by the mines of British Columbia. An examination of the statistics for the past six years will show that the supply of domestic coals imported has decreased over 30 per cent. During the same period that of the British Columbia mines has increased nearly 90 per cent, while that from distant foreign mines shows no material increase.

It may naturally be asked, why should this result follow, seeing that the abolition of the duty would apply equally to foreign coals from Great Britain and Australia, and why may not the American mines still maintain their foothold. The answer is:

1. British Columbia coal as compared with that from Washington is better for household use, and for steam purposes it equals the best and is superior to most of the local domestic products: hence, it is in greater demand in the California market.

2. British Columbia mines, having flat veins, are more cheaply worked than the pitching veins in Washington, and being nearer tide water their output can be shipped on board vessels at a lower cost than coals in Washington.

3. The product of British Columbia mines is largely carried in cheaply built and cheaply operated British steamers, and therefore the cost of freightage is less than from the American Puget Sound coal ports, that use American sailing ships and more costly steamers, and these causes have operated to diminish the California supply from Northern American coal fields, and the abolition of the present duty will finish the struggle.

With respect to distant foreign coals, the answer is: The miners of British Columbia coals sell their own product in the California markets. Controlling the amount and cost of their supplies, by the use largely of British steamers they are within four days of their mines, and are thus enabled to undertake contracts for large deliveries. The dealer in other foreign coals is distant sixty days from Australia, and one hundred and twenty to one hundred and fifty days from Great Britain. The uncertainty of the arrivals of sailing ships from such long voyages makes it inexpedient to undertake such large contracts, unless by the carriage of unwarrantably large stocks of coal. He does not know nor can he control costs, for while the free-on-board price of coal at foreign ports is practically constant, for long periods, the inward freight rates are constantly fluctuating.

Forces the American Coal out of the Market.

These are the chief reasons why the British Columbia miner is in position to force the domestic coals out of this market, and why he has been able to prevent any marked increase in importation from abroad. At the same time, while it is not contended that there should be a discriminating tariff against British Columbia, it should be emphasized that this growing absorption of California coal trade by these mines deprives the farmer of wheat-carrying vessels, tending to increase his outward wheat freights, when he competes in European markets against the world's wheat. It has retarded the mineral development of the State of Washington, which is practically in infancy, and the destruction of the tariff will further dwarf promising coal-mining in Oregon.

The Consumer Gets no Benefit by the Reduction.

Who will benefit by the reduction of the duty on coal? As the function of such laws is to do the greatest good to the masses, let us analyze the coal traffic of California, and ascertain whether the great public will reap any material advantage. The American coal-producer on the Atlantic seaboard protests against any reduction in duty, because the Nova Scotia mines will disturb his trade in the great consuming centers of New England.

The American miner on the Pacific coast contends for a chance to keep his present trade in California against mines in British Columbia, but the same kind of practical reason applicable in the East does not fit the peculiar conditions there. It can be said in prophecy that if the present duty be reduced the difference will go into the pockets of the British miner and shipownor. Theoretically it should all go to the California consumer. Practically it will not.

Iron ore of excellent quality is abundant, California alone having enough to supply the world indefinitely, but under existing conditions it is not available as a commercial factor. For our future development we are looking forward hopefully to the construction of the Nicaragua Canal to bring us in closer commercial relationship with our Southern brethren, with whom we are now working at terrible cross-purposes, hoping for the same material end. Does Alabama believe she can send her coal and iron to Italy or Turkey in exchange for figs, olives, currants, raisins, oranges, lemons, chromium, borax, or sulphur more advantageously than she could to California for the same products? All these commodities and many more are California products, in great abundance and in greater perfection than elsewhere known. Of one important thing our Eastern (including Southern) friends appear to be ignorant or indifferent and narrow: that we have all the Mediterranean countries on our Pacific coast, all Northern Europe in our Mississippi Valley, all Great Britain and her every natural resource many times repeated in our Atlantic States, all the precious mineral regions of the world in our great Western plateau, and all Scandinavia, Laplandia, and Samoldia in our Alaska. But partisanship and limited local or individual interests subordinate all to narrow dictation.

What California Pays the General Government.

The Republicans ask for this development by mutual assistance, by a syndicate of States as business men form syndicates for successful operations. We of California pay without complaint as a contribution to the general good of the other States and in support of the Government $8,000,000 of customs, of which three-quarters of a million is for coal and $2,102,581 internal revenue direct, and several millions more indirectly being paid directly at the place of manufacture of whisky, tobacco, beer, and oleo-margarine. It is estimated that California pays annually $6,000,-000 of the internal-revenue tax, when her just proportion would be less than $2,000,000, the gross amount collected in the United States being $160,296,130. Thus California pays into the Treasury over $15,000,000 annually. These great and disproportionate payments, continued through a long series of years, entitle her to careful consideration and justify her request for protection and assistance in developing her natural resources for the mutual good, power, and glory of our common country.

The Iron Industry.

There is received at the port of San Francisco from 18,000 to 22,000 long tons of pig iron annually, almost entirely from Great Britain. A little more than a year ago this trade was broken into by the arrival at that port of a shipment of 930 tons of pig iron from Birmingham, Ala. This proved of excellent quality, and more was immediately ordered. The agent, Mr. John Martin, at that time stated that the iron could be supplied at the furnaces as cheaply as at the furnaces in Scotland, but the freight rates were greatly in favor of the foreign product. That is, the rate per ton from Ensley or Birmingham via New York to San Francisco was $13.15 per ton, while from Glasgow to San Francisco the rate was $2.40 per ton. Adding to this the duty of $6.92 per ton, makes a total of $9.12 a ton, or a difference of $4.03 in favor of the British and against the Alabama product. The price of pig iron ranges in San Francisco from $3 to $30 per ton, or did at the time these transactions occurred. But with the tariff as it is and the canal of Nicaragua completed, shipments via Mobile or New Orleans to Pacific ports would place the ironworks of Alabama and other Southern States on an equality with those of Great Britain.

Here we make these concessions for mutual assistance and development. A member of the other House is reported as saying he voted against sugar because his State was not interested in sugar. Many have opposed protection to iron because, as it was charged, only one State—Pennsylvania—was engaged in its production. Now several States are interested in it, and all should be. Iron and coal are the basis of British power and wealth, and wherever in our country, under protection, their production has been carried on, there have grown prosperous communities, wealthy and powerful States. Knowing the condition of the Southern States, so undeveloped were their great natural resources when they attempted to establish the Confederacy, that a strictly enforced blockade would have soon starved the people and rendered the government powerless and compelled submission without a Bull Run, a Gettysburg, or an Appomattox. These developments are and must be through protection and interstate commerce, and not through free trade and foreign commerce.

The Income Tax.

Of the income tax, I can but say that it appears in the bill before us one of the most insidious and deceitful ever expressed in a multitude of words.

It appears most fair that the individual who rides on Mr. Bellamy's coach, which other individuals pull through the dust and mud of good and bad roads, should be made to pay his fare, or at least to pay more than those who do the pulling; and it is on this theory the income tax is advocated. Were this theory sound it would still be found impracticable to collect that fare with any equality or any degree of satisfaction or profit. At first glance it appears that the income tax is levied only against those who ride. This appearance makes the proposition popular with those who believe they do all the pulling for this coach made so famous in the "Looking Backward" story. A closer examination of these sections of the bill show that the pullers of that coach are taxed as well as those who ride.

There are but few thrifty persons who have not invested some surplus earnings or "laid aside for a rainy day" in some incorporated company or savings bank. Such people are of the most beneficial toilers of the world. They comprise millions of our people of small incomes. In all the great companies are many of these, and possibly many call for an income tax. They do not know that their savings are aggregated in the bank or other corporation, and made to pay the same tax as if the depositor's income were over the limit of four thousand. Many a poor man and woman will find their scanty dividends lessened by the income tax if this bill becomes a law.

How it Will Affect the Thrifty.

There are 4,781,605 depositors in the savings banks of the United States, with $1,712,769,026 on deposit, an average of $358.20 to each person. Of these California has 175,672 depositors, with an average of $886 of deposits, or in all $126,781,530. This includes $101,462,937 in the savings banks of San Francisco and $25,318,593 deposited in the interior savings banks of the State. How much of this belongs to "plain people," "wage-earners," and the like, it is impossible to ascertain. We know that for a long time there were many capitalists there who found it easier and more profitable to deposit large sums in savings banks than to invest themselves, but during the troubles of last year their funds were not available, and since then they are doubless withdrawing their patronage from savings banks. Many of these banks now decline to accept any large deposits, the general limit being $10,000, while some are said to have a limit of $4,000.

It stands to reason, therefore, that a very large percentage, or nearly all, of the depositors are people of moderate means, who, not being able to take care of their savings, give them into the custody of those whose business is to conduct these trusts. There are 120,642 depositors in San Francisco and 55,030 depositors in the interior banks, and while we can not get accurate statistics the nearest obtainable estimate is:

Depositors of less than $1,000	157,745
Depositors of over $1,000 and less than $2,000	8,722
Depositors of between $2,000 and $5,000	6,024
Depositors of over $5,000	3,181

The average of deposits in our four largest local savings banks in San Francisco is, viz:

German	$1,046.97
Hibernia	606.04
Savings Union	1,246.12
Savings and Loan Society	1,144.32
The lowest average deposit in all the banks is	57.67
The highest average deposit in all the banks is	1,760.00

The savings banks in California are of two classes, mutual and stock corporations, while in the East savings banks are mainly mutual concerns, having no stock, and are managed by directors more or less upon a philanthropic basis wherein all depositors are members and there are no stockholders.

Depositors In Savings Banks to Pay the Tax.

If the income tax were imposed, it would of course apply to mutual and incorporated savings banks as well as all other corporations and they would have to pay upon their income, which consists of the interest upon loans and investments. This income, less expenses and dividends to stockholders, is now used to pay interest to depositors which we will say is 5 per cent. Corporations are not so liberal as to allow this charge, the income tax, to apply entirely to stockholders; therefore it would be deducted from the 5 per cent paid depositors, and the man, who has accumulated $1,000 and is now receiving, say, $50 per annum as the earnings of his savings, would get $50, less the income tax of 2 per cent. There are also in California, and I think throughout the United States, Building and Loan associations, Mutual societies organized for the purpose of assisting the mechanic and wage-worker in building a home and paying for it in monthly installments.

Thousands of homes are by this plan builded each year, that fall like a benediction upon the American family. It is almost cruel to impose an income tax upon these societies as this law proposes.

The larger depositor, if his wealth were all in the savings banks, from which he received say $4,000 annually, would have paid the tax once through the bank and then would have to pay it again personally, and this would apply to anyone whose income was derived from corporate investments. The company would have to pay its tax and then the shareholder, who received dividends, would have to pay it again, *i. e.*, the same income or earning power would be taxed doubly in its distribution. This may be the desired object, but it is double taxation, and therefore not equitable.

Discouragement to all Enterprise.

The worst feature about the proposed measure appears to be the discouragement it would give to enterprise, and particularly to combined effort, in the form of corporate undertakings. These are the times when the greatest encouragement should be given to all who are willing to develop new resources, for so much has been done to discourage capital that disaster and misfortune appear everywhere. Is it not possible that under an income tax we would drive from us many whose wealth is now of great benefit, and should they invest their capital in other countries how could this Government collect income tax upon such investments?

A man's income is a personal affair and he will not willingly disclose it, but, if forced to, will be driven to dishonest methods in resenting what he regards as an injustice. One of the bank commissioners of California writes me:

I am told that the income tax works well in England, but I am not familiar with the system there and it may be possible that it is a blessing in disguise, but viewing it as a creation of the Democratic party, I am loath to appreciate it.

It is more or less in evidence that the rich do not pay their just share of taxes, but the proposed plan will place greater burdens upon those of moderate means, who can not escape, and the class sought to be taxed will evade the law in one way or another.

Unwise, Unnecessary, and Un-American.

I am opposed to this income tax provided for in this bill for many reasons, but first and principally because it is un-American. I am also informed there is no income-tax law proper imposed by any republic of the world to-day. It is a recognized monarchical form of taxation and should have no place upon the statute books of this country, unless as a war measure. There is no demand for it except from a few theorists and free traders who seek to secure by it money with which to pay the expenses of the Government and create an army of taxgatherers. This money, in my opinion, is needed and needed badly, but it would be more American-like if we insisted on collecting it from the foreign materials and manufactures sent here rather than from our own people. It is inquisitorial and, judging the future by the past, it will do far more to manufacture perjury than to produce an income to aid in supporting the Government. Who can deny that it is a deception; that it does not promise things it can not perform? It is supposed to be leveled at the rich and the rich alone; at those whose incomes are four thousand and over per year, and it is on its face; but there are thousands of others who will be affected by it, for it will reach into the savings banks as I have shown and tax every depositor, rich or poor.

It will affect all injuriously. It proposes also to give certain designated persons the right to look into the private business of all business men and business enterprises; to expose every one's private books to the public gaze; to require the successful business man to expose the sources of his success to those who are not so fortunate, to force him to an unnatural competition. Henry Clews, well known as a banker and financier in New York, as well as to the business world everywhere, in a recent letter says:

I remember during the war period, when various tax laws of that character were in force as war measures, it was quite a usual thing for the collector of one of the districts named, who was a bold, unscrupulous, and money-making man, to forcibly seize the books of well-known firms and keep them in his custody at his own office for experts to examine at their convenience and, I have no doubt, in many instances even to copy parts thereof; at any rate, such was the general impression.

Why it Would be Specially Injurious Now.

Hundreds of others give similar testimony. Setting aside for the present all other objections to the income-tax feature of this bill it is clear, even from the statement of the honorable chairman of the Finance Committee of this body, that it is not necessary, for the reason that the bill raises enough to meet the expenses of the Government without it. We certainly should not provide for such a great surplus of revenues as the income tax proposes to raise. We do not need it and it will turn out to be a plague to annoy and punish us. This is also the most inopportune time to try such legislation. The recent financial depression carried down many of the supposed strongest business firms and farmers of our country, and has kept them down; others who have credit have managed to keep their heads up in spite of unfavorable circumstances, and if allowed to do so will come out all right in the end.

The Danger of the Tax Gatherer.

But if they are forced to open their books and accounts to the public gaze—to the income-tax gatherers—it will be shown that they exist in many cases on credit and the confidence of their friends and supporters; and the result can not but prove disastrous to them and others. We have had enough of pulling down, and certainly there should be no excuse, no statute placed in our laws which would increase and encourage financial disaster, and which would wreck those that would otherwise sail along pleasantly until times improved, when they can manage on their own account. It is for them and those depending on them a great struggle, and if they are not required to "show their hands," as it were, they will weather the storm and sail along in pleasant waters. What we need is confidence, and it should not be destroyed by the operations of the income-tax gatherer. We have business troubles enough already staring us in the face without the law placing in their pathway one which would be even greater than all else combined.

But if this bill is to become a law there is no reason that a member of the Congress of the United States should have $4,000 of his salary that is paid him by the people go free from taxation. There should be no exemption above that of say $600 per annum, which is about the average wages of the laboring man of the country.

It has been charged by those who profess to believe that every step toward free trade is a step in the direction of national prosperity and happiness—it has been charged; I say, by these gentlemen that protection of American industries tends to build up a moneyed aristocracy at the expense of a less fortunate democracy. That is, that it tends to make the rich man richer and the poor man poorer.

Protection Does not Increase Riches at the Expense of the Poor.

I do not flatter myself that I shall be able to refute this charge with such power of eloquence and of logic that those who differ with me will at once subscribe themselves as converts to my opinion; but I must say that to me, as a business man, the facts seem to lie so distinctly in one direction, that I can not see how any other conclusion can be reached than this: that while protection has made many men rich it has made no man poor: that it has resulted and can only result in national wealth without inducing individual poverty; and that if great fortunes have been made, such fortune-making has been the logical sequence of this national prosperity, and not at the expense of the individual.

A protective tariff, as I understand it, is simply the impost of such duties as will allow the producer of this country to compete with the producer of other countries, either by keeping out entirely the products of competitive nations or by adding such amounts to their cost by a tax on entry as will enable our producer to market his goods at a fair and legitimate profit. I am aware that gentlemen of great intelligence and far more political acumen than I possess may hold this to be, if not a mistaken at least a debatable proposition; but such is my honest opinion, largely shared in, I believe, by those who are of my political faith. I know that there are gentlemen on the other side who claim that this protective tariff, while it may foster American industries, fosters them only to the benefit of the manufacturers' pocket and to the depletion of the purchasers' pocket. Now, if this were so, it would inevitably follow that the manufacturers of this country would constitute the great millionaire class. But such is not the fact.

The Value of Our Properties.

The total assessed value of all properties of the United States in the census year, 1890, I am informed, was $64,340,092,938, of which amount no less than $39,544,544,333 represent real estate and the improvements thereon: a division of our wealth in which every property owner of the United States has his share, and whose magnificent figures are due to the vast extent of our territory, to the masterly activity of our people, to their incessant desire for better surroundings, and to the general increment of values. The next largest item is that of transportation agencies; the value of railroads, street cars, shipping, canals, telegraphs, and telephones being $8,399,491,612. The magnitude of these figures, which are decidedly conservative, can hardly be said to be due to the discriminations of a protective tariff, because while the wonderful business of transportation must be undoubtedly ascribed to the movement and development of our products, we are told that the reduction of the tariff would result in an increased energy along all the lines of national and commercial affairs.

The estimated value of live stock on farms and ranges, of farm implements and machinery, is $2,703,015,040, and whether the live stock and the mechanical accessories of agriculture would be of a higher valuation if the cattle ranges and machine shops of the world could send us their yield unchecked, and whether the farmers of the country would be better therefor, is a moot and precarious question.

Our mines and quarries, including the products on hand, are valued at $1,581,964,793, and if these have been developed under a protective tariff, so much the better, and I fail to find clear or valid proof that anyone has been injured by this development.

The value of general merchandise, that is, tradesmen's stock, household and personal effects, grain in elevators, goods in bond, and all exempt State and national properties is $7,893,708,821.

There remain to be noticed only the estimated value of the machinery and the product on hand of mills and factories, $3,058,593,441, and the gold and silver coin and bullion, $1,158,-774,948; and it seems to me absurd to seriously advance or combat the proposition that the effect of a protective tariff has been to place either of these two amounts in the centralized control of a few rich men to the detriment of the many poor.

Let us look a little more particularly into this fascinating subject of accumulated riches. That we have a moneyed aristocracy can not be denied, but I find nothing in its composition to show that it has been built up by a protective tariff; nothing that would even indirectly point to that inference. New York to-day, I suppose, contains more rich men than any other city in the world, but its lists of plutocrats is singularly deficient in those millionaire manufacturers who, we are told, have sprung up in the hotbed culture of protection.

How Riches Have Been Piled Up.

The rich men of the West have rolled up millions in railroads and mines, and those of the Central and Southern States chiefly through the manipulation or ownership of agricultural products and live stock. I might add the names of the many millionaire women, rich through shrewd investments, but refrain from introducing them in this discussion. It is a far more difficult task, I find, to start on a list of manufacturers who enjoy a parity of wealth with those I have referred to, and a still more difficult one to trace any connection between their wealth and the protective tariff. Some, it is true, have built up fortunes more or less vast in manufacturing, but it is equally true that they have made these fortunes under the protection of patents and not under the protection of tariff. And these patents upon new inventions have resulted in most every instance in reducing the price of the manufactured articles to the public.

I am aware that the great manufacturing States of the East contain hundreds and thousands of men who have reached opulence through the prosecution of protected industries, but their opulence is a comparative one and not that of the great rich ones of the nation who through real estate, railroads, trusts, and speculation in man's avidity for sudden gain really control the financial balance of the country. This general statement is borne out in an especially forcible way by the detailed facts collected some little time ago by a New York newspaper. A census was at that time taken of all the millionaires in the United States, and a schedule furnished of the source of their wealth.

An actual list of 4,047 persons reputed to be worth a million dollars or more was compiled—of whom, by the bye, no fewer than 1,103 lived in New York City—and the recapitulation of the sources of wealth displayed a very curious and instructive condition of things.

The Sources of Wealth.

The condensed history of these 4,000 showed that 986 have made their fortunes in merchandising; 188 in mines and mining; 436 in railroads, shipping, and other transportation agencies; 803 in real estate, banking, and kindred occupations; 75 in agricultural pursuits; 93 in patented and proprietary articles; 58 in brokerage; 76 in local investments; 178 in such miscellaneous industries as contracts, hotel-keeping, etc.; 55 through indefinite sources; 65 in law practice, and 1 in that of medicine; 57 in printing and publishing; 357 in such indirectly protected industries as sugar-refining, tobacco-growing, malting, milling, etc.; and 619 in protected manufactures. Thus, from still another set of figures, the same unerring deductions are to be drawn, that a protective tariff is not the cause of the uneven distribution of wealth; that the accretion of great riches is due to the varied causes of temperament, inheritance, fortune, invention, shrewdness, and the rewards of commercial integrity; and that unless the accumulation of riches can be shown to be an evil, the list of millionaires can scarcely be classed as an exemplification of malign laws. There are yet other statistics at command which lift the proposition at issue far above the uncertain limits of hypothesis.

The $3,058,593,441 which I quoted from the stock account of the wealth of the nation represent, it will be remembered, the estimated value of the manufacturers' plant and stock on hand June 30, 1890, while late census figures show that the value of the manufactured products of the United States for the year ending June 30, 1890, was $9,370,107,624—truly a magnificent figure. Yes, but let us look for a moment at its components and distribution. In the first place, the cost of the material was no less than $5,158,868,353, which leaves the net addition to the wealth of the country at $4,211,239,271. Now, what does this sum represent? It represents the wages of the operative, the salary of the clerks, the premium to the artist, the payments on borrowed money, the interest on invested capital, contributions to government, local, State, and national; outlay for wear and tear, insurance, extension of plant, and, sometimes, profit.

The Sums Paid the Workers.

The wage account is an interesting one. To 106,620 clerks
there was paid $117,574,355, while to all other employés, num-
bering 4,250,783, there was paid $1,830,903,747, or a total of
$2,005,483,102. A simple sum in division will show us that the
clerks received an average of a little over $1,100 per annum,
while the army of workmen and workwomen and workchildren
received an average of nearly $445 per annum. It seems to me
that this one group of facts alone settles it that the people—the
working people—are they who live and flourish under the benefits of protection. The people, indeed, for it should not be for-
gotten that the workers to whom the $2,005,483,102 was paid in
wages numbered 4,357,403, or one-fifteenth of the entire population of the United States. Nor do these figures take into note
the foundries, the machine shops, the architects, contractors,
carpenters, and builders, whose services and labors are required
as the industry grows; nor the factors and middlemen, nor the
hundred and one more or less indirect beneficiaries of the industry. And it is God's blessing that it is so; and it has been our
country's blessing and pride that it is so; and we should be careful indeed how we approach the momentous matter of change,
and how we warp or modify a condition that has been so pro-
ductive of general benefit.

The Intricacies of the Tariff.

No man has a greater appreciation of the intricacies of the tariff
than I, nor has any man a better appreciation than I of the ex-
ceeding presumption that would mark any attempt on my part
to simplify these intricacies. But it sometimes happens that the
tyro may single out one proposition which seem likely to escape
attention in a general discussion and which may be plainly and
pertinently answered by the rules of common sense and business
experience. It is to such a proposition that I have ventured to
address myself, and it is in such a manner that I have ventured
to specially refer to this phase of the subject under discussion.

We rejoice in the general prosperity of the world—all the nations of the earth. We feel a fraternal interest in the people of
our own continent who have struggled with us in establishing
free governments. We seek by legislation to advance the interests of our own country. In this can we not follow in the
path and emulate the deeds of that grand statesman my native
State proudly claimed as her own, and who did more than any
other to inculcate these doctrines of protection and reciprocity
for the good of our land and for sealing the friendships of all our
American republics? To him we owe so much and returned so
little—he who, standing on the sea-beaten cliffs of Maine, where
the morning sun first sheds its beams on our most eastern shore,
gazed over the land he loved with every thought of fostering
care: over the hills and factories of New England, the great me-
tropolis with its radiating arms of commerce, the rugged masses
of the Appalachian chain with their stores of mineral wealth, the
long Atlantic coast indented with its many harbors, bays and rivers; over the fair fields, forests, and orange groves of the South-
land, the broad valley of the Mississippi from the great unsalted
seas and the countless sparkling lakes of the north to the distant
Gulf of Mexico, with all the teeming industries of farms, and mines,

and manufactures, and trade of State with State; on over the empire of plains, the lofty Rocky Mountains, seamed with veins of glittering gold and silver; over the high plateaus and the snow-crowned ridge of the golden Sierra, with the genial and fruitful land at its base: on to the Pacific and the islands of the sea; on to the wild shores of Alaska—all his own great country, whose every locality he knew, whose every resource he fostered, whose every interest he guarded with a heart too large for sectionalism, a mind too pure for prejudice, let us, as he, take the broad views, be true and just to all, include all in our embrace, from Maine to California. Dirigo and Eureka!

1257

www.ingramcontent.com/pod-product-compliance
Lightning Source LLC
Chambersburg PA
CBHW021548270326
41930CB00008B/1418